Health Essentials

Chi Kung

James MacRitchie is from Liverpool, in north-west England. His early background was in the contemporary Arts – Painting, Rock'n'Roll, Community Arts, Choreography and Alternative Theatre. James previously co-authored *The State Of Play – Theatre Games as Social Art* with Bill Harpe, and *Exit to Enter – Dance as a Process for Personal and Artistic Growth* with Anna Halprin. He co-founded and co-directed The Natural Dance Workshop in London and Europe (1975–81), and The Evolving Institute in Boulder, Colorado (1982–88).

James has been a Classical Acupuncturist since 1977 and has been practising, studying and teaching body-energy and Chi Kung for ten years. He was Founding President of The Acupuncture Association of Colorado. He now directs The Body-Energy Center in Boulder, Colorado, with his wife Damaris Jarboux – a centre concerned with understanding the anatomy and physiology of the Energy-Body, and its relationship to the Soul and the Spirit.

James has wide experience in public speaking, teaching and leading workshops and events.

The Health Essentials Series

There is a growing number of people who find themselves attracted to holistic or alternative therapies and natural approaches to maintaining optimum health and vitality. The *Health Essentials* series is designed to help the newcomer by presenting high quality introductions to all the main complementary health subjects. Each book presents all the essential information on each therapy, explaining what it is, how it works and what it can do for the reader. Advice is also given, where possible, on how to begin using the therapy at home, together with comprehensive lists of courses and classes available worldwide.

The *Health Essentials* titles are all written by practising experts in their fields. Exceptionally clear and concise, each text is supported by attractive illustrations.

Series Medical Consultant
Dr John Cosh, MD, FRCP

In the same series

Acupuncture by Peter Mole
Alexander Technique by Richard Brennan
Aromatherapy by Christine Wildwood
Ayurveda by Scott Gerson MD
Chinese Medicine by Tom Williams
Colour Therapy by Pauline Wills
Flower Remedies by Christine Wildwood
Herbal Medicine by Vicki Pitman
Kinesiology by Ann Holdway
Massage by Stewart Mitchell
Reflexology by Inge Dougans with Suzanne Ellis
Shiatsu by Elaine Liechti
Skin and Body Care by Sidra Shaukat
Spiritual Healing by Jack Angelo
Vitamin Guide by Hasnain Walji

Health Essentials

CHI KUNG

cultivating personal energy

JAMES MACRITCHIE

B.Ac. (UK), Dipl. Ac. (NCCA)

ELEMENT

Shaftesbury, Dorset • Rockport, Massachusetts

Brisbane, Queensland

First published in Great Britain in 1993 by
Element Books Limited
Shaftesbury, Dorset SP7 8BP

Published in the USA in 1993 by
Element Books, Inc.
PO Box 830, Rockport, MA 01966

Published in Australia in 1993 by
Element Books Limited for
Jacaranda Wiley Limited
33 Park Road, Milton, Brisbane 4064

Reprinted February and August 1995

Cover design by Max Fairbrother
Designed by Nancy Lawrence
Typeset by The Electronic Book Factory Ltd, Fife, Scotland
Printed and bound in Great Britain by
Biddles Ltd, Guildford & King's Lynn

British Library Cataloguing in Publication
Data available

Library of Congress Cataloging in Publication Data
MacRitchie, James
Chi kung: cultivating personal energy
James MacRitchie
1. Chi kung. I. Title II. Series
RA781.8 M33 1993
613.7'1 dc20

ISBN 1–85230–371–9

Note from the Publisher

Any information given in any book in the *Health Essentials* series is not intended to be taken as a replacement for medical advice. Any person with a condition requiring medical attention should consult a qualified medical practitioner or suitable therapist.

Contents

Author's Note		viii
Preface		1
Chi Kung Practices to Experience Your Own Chi		7
1.	What is Chi Kung?	9
2.	The Story of Chi Kung	25
3.	Oriental Energy – Anatomy and Physiology	45
4.	The Different Kinds of Chi Kung and Their Applications	70
5.	How Does Chi Kung Relate to other Body-Energy Systems?	89
6.	Chi Kung and You	104
Summary of Exercises		118
Bibliography		121
Glossary		125
Further Information		129
Index		135

This book is dedicated with my love,
to my mother,
Joan Frederica Tilley,
and to my son,
John Michael.

ACKNOWLEDGEMENTS

My heartfelt 'Thanks' and deep appreciation to all of the people who helped make this project possible.

To my wonderful wife, Damaris Jarboux, and my step-children Sonnet and Hagan, for their understanding, patience, support and love.

To Eddie and Debbie Shapiro, for initially asking me to write this book. To Susan Mears, who originally commissioned the book, for her inspiration and advice. To Julia McCutchen, the Senior Commissioning Editor at Element, for guiding me along the way. To Valerie Finlay, David Alexander, Maureen, Lisa, and the staff of Element Books for their assistance, and especially to Michael Mann for making it all possible.

To the numerous teachers, practitioners, publishers and resource people who most kindly gave their time and assistance on this project. Rather than list them here they are listed in the Useful Addresses Section, at the end of the book. My sincerest appreciation.

To the following who gave their encouragement and help: Mark Barasch, Francis Butler, Prof. Da-Li Feng, Rick Fields, Pao-Chin Huang, George Leonard, Chia Lu, Kent Nuzum, Bob Pasternak, Sharon Pierson, Richard Ruster, David Scott, Mike Sigman, Michael Winn, Bill Wiswell, Corey Wong . . . and anybody else I have forgotten to mention.

Special thanks to my various teachers: Bruce Mitchell for showing me how to do the gig, Bill and Wendy Harpe for demonstrating social responsibility, Anna Halprin for unlocking creativity, Prof. J.R. Worsley and Dr Judy Becker Worsley for teaching compassion, and Dr. Robert B. McFarland for illuminating the power of conviction and humour in adversity.

To my assistant, Cyndy de Chelly (Rogers), for her many contributions, and for making it all easier.

For reading the manuscript in its various evolutions: Carolyn Stollman, Judy Jacobsen, Jesse Dammann, Brenda Allen, Farokh Omid, Laura Barnard, Elisabeth Culley, Diane Warren, Gary Ferrini and Brian Van Duzee.

Thank You

EXERCISE CREDITS

The exercises of 'The Healing Smile' and 'Focusing At Your Body-Energy Centre' are adapted from the teachings of Master Mantak Chia.

The exercises of 'The Energy Shower' and 'Energy Re-charge' are adapted from teachings of Master Liang, Shou-Yu.

The exercise 'Healing Energy In Your Hands' is from teachings of Damaris Jarboux.

The exercise 'Knocking At The Gate Of Life' is a well-known practise.

PICTURE CREDITS

Page 56: Union of the Three Treasures
Illustration from *Hsing Ming Kwei Chr/The Law of Nature and Destiny*. Reprinted from the 'T'ien Tao Correspondence Program', published by the Chinese National Chi Kung Institute, Inc. By kind permission of Roger D. Hagood.

Page 86: Tang Dynasty Internal Body View
Illustration from a seventh–tenth century AD stone carving from a Taoist Monastery. Adapted by Mark Johnson, and used with his kind permission.

AUTHOR'S NOTE

Chi Kung is the name for a variety of exercises and meditations which, if performed correctly and under appropriate supervision, can greatly benefit your health and well-being. It should be taken seriously and is not to be 'played with'. If performed incorrectly these practices can cause undesirable effects. It is important to follow the general guidelines in practising the introductory exercises in this book. Also please pay attention to the recommendations regarding finding a good teacher.

The exercises in this book are not intended as a substitute for medical treatment. In case of medical concerns please consult a medical doctor.

The opinions expressed in this book are my own, and have grown out of my own practice and experience of Chi Kung, fifteen years of practising classical Taoist acupuncture, and the research, understanding and interpretations gathered during the compilation of this material. They are not intended to represent anything other than this, and are presented as my own personal point of view – as a student, observer and commentator – of this newly emerging body of knowledge.

In no way do I wish for these opinions to be misinterpreted as any kind of final authorative statement or conclusion about Chi Kung; there are many Chi Kung Masters and all manner of styles and traditions going back thousands of years. I do, however, hope that this book makes a contribution in the understanding of Chi Kung as it enters the West. I also most sincerely hope that this book serves to inform you and inspire you to find a teacher, and to begin to do this tremendously valuable practice yourself.

Preface

IN 1973 I WAS taking part in a dance workshop in California. After twelve very intense, full days with a couple of dozen people from across the country, the last day concluded with a row of conga drummers pounding out a beat throughout the afternoon, and the whole studio was filled with furiously dancing bodies. These people had been dancing for four hours. I was wrapped up in a blanket in the corner – exhausted, withdrawn, recuperating. A question suddenly and unexpectedly appeared in my mind, a question that has motivated and driven me ever since: 'Where does the energy come from . . . and how does it work?'

Later, after returning home to England, I gradually realized that energy was considered by some people to be at the very basis of their health and well-being, while others held it in such high regard that it was the foundation of their spiritual life. Other questions began to emerge:

- How do you experience and feel your own energy?
- How does energy underlie your health and well-being?
- What can you do to get your energy to its best?

It seemed that these simple questions held the magical key to the quality and essence of life: how you live it, how you feel it and your everyday experience.

Being an ordinary working-class lad from Liverpool, in the north of England, I just wanted some simple, straightforward answers, so that I could figure this stuff out, charge up my energy whenever I wanted to and get on with life. However, there was nothing in simple English, written by or for the ordinary person, that made much sense. Energy is at the foundation of many aspects of ourselves, and yet most curiously, when I began to look at what was available in the way of studying it there was very little understandable information. A very curious state of affairs indeed! Yoga seemed to be a comprehensive system, but its style did not attract me.

Also having spent the previous ten years of life involved in the Arts, the Rock'n'Roll business and Community Theatre, I faced the usual issue for someone in his mid-twenties of what to do with the rest of one's life. After looking at all of the options it seemed that one move was to learn about this fundamental stuff called energy by studying a particular energy system – to learn the science and the anatomy and physiology of it all, and how to use it. I enrolled in acupuncture school.

At the same time I also began teaching dance, working with body-energy as expression, creativity and personal development. This unexpectedly took on a life of its own, and flowered into *The Natural Dance Workshop*, using non-stylized dance – which everybody could do – with humanistic psychology and group process as a form of social art. Initially based in London this work later expanded into Europe and became established as a new form of dance. After graduating from acupuncture school I practised part-time in London.

Acupuncture is a complete and comprehensive body of knowledge about the energy system, rooted in the depths of Oriental philosophy. But acupuncture itself, the use of hair-fine needles and heat, is simply a method or technique for affecting energy in the body, and it became obvious that there was more to understanding energy than one particular method. There was some deeper level of understanding, but nobody seemed to know much about it.

In 1981 I returned to live in the United States, in Boulder, Colorado – mainly to concentrate on and pursue the practice of acupuncture and the investigation and understanding of energy – and towards this end co-established with Anna Wise *The Evolving Institute : A Center for Personal and Social Evolution*.

One morning in 1983 I was innocently sitting at my desk minding my own business and going through the mail. I opened a leaflet. It announced a weekend workshop in 'Chi Kung'. 'Chi What?!' I gasped. My mind flashed off and on a number of times, then short-circuited. Over the previous nine years I had been involved in acupuncture and Oriental medicine, belonged to professional societies, was affiliated with the Alternative Health and New Age movements, had attended international conferences . . . Not once had I heard the name Chi Kung even mentioned. Maybe this was 'It'!

That weekend I entered through a magic doorway which changed the direction of my life and took it into a new dimension. I met my first Chi Kung teacher, Master Mantak Chia. After training extensively myself I began to teach patients and others some of these methods and procedures for experiencing and controlling their own energy and since that time I have met and studied with a variety of teachers and practitioners. Chi Kung has become integrated into my life as my personal practice, to my own great benefit. Fifteen years of Taoist acupuncture practice on a daily basis has provided a solid foundation for working with, and understanding, chi. Teaching classes over the last eight years has now grown into a variety of comprehensive training programmes.

However, as we shall see, Chi Kung is only one approach to working with energy in the body. With an eye on the larger picture of body-energy in all of its aspects, and its social and cultural relevance, in 1989 I established, with my wife Damaris Jarboux, *The Body-Energy Center* in Boulder, Colorado. We are concerned with understanding the anatomy and physiology of the Energy-Body, and its relationship to the health of the Body, the Soul and the Spirit. We integrate Chi Kung with acupuncture, therapeutic touch and other modalities, in private practice, training and workshops. We also use traditional and contemporary knowledge, along with ritual forms and myths, as ways of stimulating personal and group process. With a major concern for the significance of this work in the larger social and cultural context, we organize conferences, community activities and hold large-scale participatory dance events.

This book will introduce you to a field of knowledge which has only just, in the historical blinking of an eye, become available in the West. However, over the course of recorded history – three thousand years and 120 generations – an ever-increasing body of knowledge about our energy has been developing in China and the Orient. It is the basis of their health care, their spiritual development and their daily life. Emperors, monks, doctors, martial artists and others have learned how to generate, control, develop, refine, purify and store their own energy, and even transmit it to others. It has been kept secret, passed down verbally from teacher to student and reserved for the most favoured and privileged, but now, in the new global information age, this most wonderful knowledge has grown to the stage where it is becoming available to everyone. In mainland China it is said that there is now a 'Chi Kung Craze'. In 1988, in Beijing, there was 'The First World Conference for Academic Exchange of Medical Qigong', in which 128 international presenters gave papers and demonstrations ranging from scientific and medical research to comparisons with Buddhist and Yoga higher states of consciousness. In 1990 'The First International Congress of Qigong' took place in Berkeley, California, during which the 1990s were named 'The Qigong Decade'. Other such conferences have since taken place, and more are planned. In China, the dragon is an ancient symbol of spiritual re-finement. Now, the dragon is out of the bag.

The name 'Chi Kung' needs some comment at this point. In research for this book I was told that the word Chi Kung is a recent name given to these practices earlier this century. This name is also spelt in other ways, which you may be more familiar with. Chi Kung comes from the Wade-Giles transliteration system of Chinese-English. In recent years the Chinese government have established their own transliteration of Chinese into English, known as Pin Yin, therefore a common spelling now used is Qi Gong or Qigong. Another transliteration is Chi Gung. I have used Chi Kung throughout the text, except where Qi Gong is used as a proper noun, because it reflects the older Taoist tradition and also because I personally like the look and sound of it better. However, please spell it for yourself in whichever way is right for you.

Historically the names used for the practices were Dao Yin (Dao = breathing, Yin = physical movements), Tu Na (Expiration and Inspiration) and Tugu Naxin (Tugu = getting rid of the stale, Naxin = taking in the fresh).

At the back of the book is a glossary of terms with their variations and meanings. The Chinese language is open to various translations and interpretations into English; words are written differently by different writers. In reading other sources you may come across completely different English spellings of the same word, to the extent that at first glance it may not even be recognizable as the same word. There is no standardized system of transliteration, because the sources are so disparate, so you are advised to read carefully and make your own correlations.

When the idea of writing this book was first proposed in 1990, the initial question was how to gather the information for research.

There was very little information easily available and no commonly agreed source or single reference. In talking with various teachers and publishers I realized that to compile this information adequately it would be necessary to approach it as investigative journalism; talk to as many people as possible and begin to put the pieces together.

This book is the result of personal interviews with Chi Kung teachers, dozens of books, innumerable phone conversations, visits and discussions with writers and publishers, surveys, a trip to England, magazines, articles, training manuals . . . Part of this research involved the ever-increasing number of books on Chi Kung which simultaneously began appearing in the mid-1980s. (For some inexplicable reason four authors independently published their first books in English in 1985!) However, the majority of these books appear to appeal to the already converted – acupuncturists, Tai Chi Chuan practitioners, martial artists and other students of Chinese culture. These are listed in the Bibliography at the back of the book for your further reference and information.

This book is an attempt to describe Chi Kung in simple straightforward terms, in a common language that everybody can understand. It has been an education, and a labour of love, and during the research and writing I have been privileged to meet some of the most remarkable and impressive people of my life.

If Chi Kung is new to you this book may help get you pointed in the right direction. It is a personal interpretation and report of the current state of this emerging field. It has been written with three audiences in mind:

- As an introductory guide for the layperson to inform people that are new to Chi Kung.
- For the Chi Kung student, to outline the scope and range of practice.
- For Chi Kung teachers as another way of presenting it in our Western context.

It begins with an introduction to what Chi Kung is and how it works, followed by an outline of its history and development. The text then describes the energy anatomy and physiology which underlies Chi Kung, shows the various applications and ways in which Chi Kung can be used, and looks at its relationship to other body-energy systems. Finally, it discusses how Chi Kung relates to your everyday life. At the end of each chapter there is a series of exercises which you can do yourself, to experience your own energy.

If Chi Kung is new to you I hope that this book will inspire you to find a teacher and begin practice. If you are already a practitioner I hope that it will help you extend and continue further.

Chi Kung is one of the most important and fundamental practices that you can do. Over the last thirty years, acupuncture, and the concepts and reality of Oriental body-energy, have hit the West like a tidal wave, and are now commonplace. The same is happily about to happen, to everyone's benefit, with Chi Kung. I most sincerely hope that this book inspires you to find out more, to begin practice and to cultivate and develop that most essential and important part of yourself – your energy.

James MacRitchie
Boulder, Colorado, 1992

Chi Kung Practices To Experience Your Own Chi

TO MAKE THIS more than just a theoretical book we have included a series of exercises for you to do, so that you can get an experience of what is being written about, and of your own chi/energy.

At the end of each chapter there is a sequence of practical exercises which you can do yourself. These six exercises have been selected to give you a basic introduction to what is involved. All of these exercises can be done by anyone in an average state of health – whatever your age or previous experience. They are also accumulative, and develop one from the other.

Follow the instructions in a general way. They are not absolutely rigid, but should be followed as to their obvious intent. They are in the following sequence:

1. *The Healing Smile*
   Learn to smile at your own internal organs, release tension and generate relaxation.
2. *The Energy Shower*
   Draw external chi into you, and use it to clean out negative energy and refresh you.
3. *Focusing at Your Body Energy Centre*
   Concentrate your chi into your Centre Place, and store it there.
4. *Knocking at The Door of Life*
   Activate the deep level of your ancestral energy.
5. *Energy Re-charge*
   Use these postures to generate strength, and learn how to direct your own energy inside yourself.

6. *Healing Energy in Your Hands*
   How to generate and accumulate your own energy and use it to heal yourself, and others.

These exercises have been selected from various sources, and adapted and designed to give you an introductory experience of Chi Kung. They are intended to be useful to you at any time, as, and when, they are needed, but first you have to learn them. To begin, read through the instructions thoroughly. Then try them out, and repeat them slowly until you begin to get the general idea and intention. Then try them on your own without referring to the instructions. To practise it is advisable to wear comfortable, loose-fitting clothes, with nothing binding at the waist.

Because of the inherent difficulty involved in reading instructions whilst simultaneously practising it may be helpful if you begin by having somebody else read them out to you as you perform them, or try speaking the instructions into a tape recorder, then play it back to guide you in practice until you learn it yourself. Take it slowly and easily.

To aid in these practices an audio cassette tape has been produced by the author to guide you through these exercises, details of which are listed in the Useful Information section at the back of the book.

Each of these exercises is accumulative with the previous ones. If you learn each one you can then practise them all continuously, in the order presented, and this whole sequence will cleanse and tonify your energy, refresh and energize you or you can mix and match them as you wish. Try it and see. Once you learn these practices, you will have them available to you for the rest of your life. Learn these simple exercises and practise them regularly and you will own one of the best forms of preventive medicine that humankind has ever developed. This has to be one of the best deals anywhere – such enormous benefit for such little effort. It is truly an investment in your health and yourself.

Learn these practices. Do them till you feel your chi. You will be rewarded a thousandfold for your efforts.

1

What is Chi Kung?

CHI KUNG COVERS a vast territory. It is such a broad umbrella term that it can be compared to someone from China coming to the West to study. You ask her what she is here for, and with wide-eyed enthusiasm she proudly announces 'I am here to study *Music*!' The obvious next question would be, of course, what kind of music? Just as there are many kinds of music so there are many kinds of Chi Kung. I have been told that there are 1,000 different Chi Kungs, even 10,000. What can this mean?

Fig. 1. Chi Kung

It is now familiar to many people in the West – thanks to acupuncture, Tai Chi Chuan and martial arts – that 'Chi' means 'energy'. But 'Kung' is a term for which there is no easily familiar equivalent in the West that is part of our everyday frame of reference – and yet it is at the foundation of much of Chinese culture! 'Kung' translates best into the word 'cultivation'.

Over the last twenty-five years we have become accustomed to the popular use of the terms Personal Development, Personal Growth and Self-Discovery; indeed, following the flowering of Humanistic Psychology and the Human Potential Movement these have become major criteria that people aspire to. But 'cultivation' has a different edge to it. It is not in tune with the normal Western attitude to life. It is not fast. It is not fashionable. It is not glamorous. It denotes something which is slow and steady and gradual and constant and humble. It requires a different frame of mind from the one we usually have. It takes time. It means doing something long term in a committed and dedicated way. One of the best descriptions is that cultivating your energy through regular practice is like putting one piece of paper on top of another – over time you have a tower the size and strength of a skyscraper. This is what Chi Kung practitioners are doing – cultivating energy, and thereby practising Personal Cultivation.

WHY DO CHI KUNG?

So why do Chi Kung when it seems like such a commitment for such a long time? What would you want to do it for anyway?

The simplest reason is because it makes you feel good! (I don't know anybody in their right mind who would rather feel bad than good.)

But what does feeling good mean?

It means health, well-being, emotional clarity and balance, being grounded, a desirable state of being, feeling integrated, sensitive, clear-minded, happiness, satisfaction, accessing your higher self, spiritual development . . . You name it, and in some way or other it can probably be achieved, or improved, through practising Chi Kung.

There are many ways in which this can be experienced:

- It may be subjective sensations such as feeling bright-eyed, clear-headed, high-spirited, euphoric, at perfect peace, completely relaxed, deeply refreshed and other positive and desirable sensations.

- It may be in purely physical terms, such as increased stamina, better digestion, improved circulation, increased resistance to illness, less tiredness and fatigue.

- It may serve to eliminate problems and symptoms – some of which can be very specific, and others that you never knew you had until they went away.

In China it is said that Chi Kung can be practised for curing illness, prevention of disease, strengthening the constitution, avoiding premature aging and prolonging life. The Chinese are modest people and have no history of capitalist marketing, promotion and hype. If the Chinese had invented Coca-Cola it would be described something like 'a nice-tasting drink which gives refreshment' – and nobody would know about it. They certainly wouldn't say 'Coke is IT!' in flashing fluorescent neon.

So consider for a moment or two the meaning of these statements:

- *Curing Illness*: the significance of this is relevant to everyone. It could provide a revolution in medicine and health care, to everybody's benefit.

- *Prevention of Disease*: this could be the much sought-after preventative treatment that will keep you in sound good health.

- *Strengthening the Constitution*: developing a strong foundation of health is a common concern – witness the obsession with fitness, health clubs, exercise, sports.

- *Avoiding Premature Aging*: everybody ages, it's one of the rules, but *nobody* wants to age any faster than they can possibly avoid.

- *Prolonging Life*: most people in reasonable health want to enjoy life as long as possible.

And the above is actually a modest list! There's much more to it than that – gaining personal power, developing extra-ordinary abilities, entering into heightened states of consciousness, living in blissfulness . . . Translate the usual prosaic Chinese statements into contemporary Western terms and it is inconceivable what advertisers could come up with.

So, why do Chi Kung? Because it is one of the best things that you can possibly do for yourself.

THE SPECTRUM OF CHI KUNGS

There is a wide spectrum of Chi Kung. It is, in fact, such a broad, generic term that it is almost meaningless. What you really want to know is 'what kind of Chi Kung?' There are very ancient

Chi Kung forms which have been transmitted faithfully through the generations, and there are forms which are being invented today; there are special styles which are family secrets that only get passed down through the males (because a female will probably get married and then her allegiance and commitment is to her new husband and his family, along with everything she knows). And there are traditional forms which have been elaborated upon, added to, changed and expanded almost beyond recognition until it seems that everyone has his or her own version of it; for instance The Five Animal Frolics and The Six Healing Sounds.

It is a point of pride that a teacher will tell you that he/she has developed his/her own style. In fact, I have never met a teacher who has taught in a way which was similar to any other teacher. Everyone seems to do it differently. Everyone has their own individual style. Some forms are named after the originator, as in Yan Xin Qigong, Lianggong Shr Ba Fa and The Chow Integrated Healing System which were developed by Master Yan Xin, Master Liang Shou-Yu and Master Effie Poy Yew Chow. Other teachers have created tradenames for their style, as in 'The Healing Tao' of Master Mantak Chia, or formed their own organizations, such as Dr Yang Jwing-Ming's 'Yang's Martial Arts Association'. All of these Chinese teachers are currently living in North America. However, like travelling different routes to get to the same destination, it may be that all of the various forms and styles get to the same place in the end!

How can this be? Well, taking a familiar comparison from our own contemporary culture – how many ways are there to play 'The Blues'? The Blues are a particular and very specific popular musical form which is essentially based on playing only three chords. However, the various possibilities of progressions and variations of playing just these three chords has led to literally thousands of musicians and bands who only play 'The Blues', each with their own very individual and distinct style; and tens, if not hundreds, of thousands of different tunes and songs – all based on the same simple principle and structure. This is one of the most obvious examples of 'Variations On A Theme'. It is similar in Chi Kung.

Another familiar comparison is playing the piano. There are only a limited number of ways of playing the piano – there are the same notes and chords available for everyone – but some people play for angelic choirs, some play classics, some play hyper-sophisticated jazz, some play music you can whistle while you work and others play in such a way that they drive you out of the room. Everyone seems to do it differently, and, in fact, in the West if somebody sounds too much like someone else they can get ridiculed – or even sued!

One of the major problems is that there are aspects of our attitudes and expectations which are culturally conditioned and ingrained. We take these attitudes for granted and are unable to see them clearly; for most people they only stretch to the horizon of their own lifetime. We are limited and contained within our own culturally myopic context and it is difficult to see and appreciate how life must have been in ancient China. For instance, if you want to find out about something your first instinct is probably to go and get a book on it. You go to the library, get out the standard reference book and look it up. This is all well and good, except for one consideration – it is particular to this present era, and it depends upon having commonly agreed standards of reference.

Compare this to ancient China. There, just as in ancient Europe, there were no telephones, faxes, broadcast channels or video training tapes. There weren't even any bookstores you could just wander into and browse. China up until the communist revolution, half-way through this century, has been well described as 'High Medieval'. Things hadn't really changed much for a long time. Tradition ruled.

One consequence of this, essential to understanding Chi Kung, is that there were no commonly agreed standards (there was no more a 'right' way to do Chi Kung than there was a 'right' way to dance). Another major conditioning fact was that of geographical isolation. The country was too vast and primitive to allow for much communication and exchange, so not much got passed around. Chi Kung is essentially a non-verbal activity taught individually person to person, like dance, and so it was passed on very slowly. Such a tradition limits knowledge and practice to the initiated, and avoids the dangers of misinterpretation inherent in books. Also, to complicate matters further, there was a deeply embedded cultural attitude that you kept such knowledge, skills and information to yourself, and it was fiercely and jealously guarded; only to be passed on to your own children, your most favourite ones or the most deserving. Even if it did appear in writing, it was heavily cloaked in symbolic and metaphorical language.

Given all these factors, all manner of different and diverse forms and styles developed and evolved for all kinds of reasons, and, of course, everyone thought that their way was the 'right' way and was 'best'. But how does all this relate to you and your ordinary life?

CHI KUNG AND YOUR EVERYDAY LIFE

Practising Chi Kung in a meditation hall with a view of the timeless snow-covered mountains going through their subtle changes of brightness and colour as clouds and sunshine and mist and blue sky come and go is a most desirable activity. But how does this relate to living in the twentieth century, going to work every day, driving around in an upholstered armchair at sixty miles an hour, getting dinner cooked, eaten and cleaned up, maintaining relationships with everyone in your life including yourself, taking care of the kids . . . trying to get everything to work in balance including the money going out being somewhere in the region of money coming in. How is Chi Kung relevant to all this? This is a good question! I thought you might wonder that.

Well, it all seems to relate to what it is that you want, and why and how you want it.

Given that we are all living individually with all of our own peculiarities, eccentricities, pressures and delights there are also some things that we all share by virtue of being human. Just as we all have the same bones and bone structure, but which are individually shaped, we also have the same kind of energy system. We also have very similar desires, wants and needs.

One thing that everybody seems to want, at least everyone that I have met so far, is health. I have never met anybody who wanted to be sick.

Now one of the peculiar things about health is that in the West nobody seems to know what it is, yet here we are with a concern that affects everybody, and which has grown to a size that constitutes an 'industry' – The Health Care Industry. In the United States at least (and probably most other places) it is second in size only to the Defence Industry and the annual expenditure on health is around 750 billion dollars per year. That is three-quarters of a trillion dollars.

The first thing one might conclude from these figures is that people are incredibly healthy in the US. They are not. They are nowhere near as healthy as the Chinese, and comparatively the Chinese have nothing at all. However the most astonishing and absurd thing, given these numbers, is that:

In the West we do not have a measurable definition of health.

That is such an important and unbelievable statement that it bears repeating.

In the West we do not have a measurable definition of health.

Unbelievable as it is, we do not have a way of defining and measuring the state of health. There is no medical text book which defines the state of health. There is no monitoring process for when, and how much, we are healthy. We only know when we are unhealthy, because then something is wrong. The working definition of health in Western medicine is when you are not ill. Well, thanks a million, but by then I'm already sick; it's too late. It's not like closing the door after the horse has bolted; it's not even knowing where the barn is!

In the West when someone is ill we ask 'What is wrong with this person?' and then go about doing whatever it is that we do to track down the cause of the sickness and cure it, destroy it, remove it, replace it or whatever else seems appropriate according to the current level of medical science.

In China, this whole proposition is reversed. They simply turn it around. When someone is ill they ask the simple question 'Why is this person not healthy?' *Because if they were healthy they wouldn't be ill.* Incredibly, they just ask the question differently . . . and save hundreds of billions of dollars.

Now I, for one, think that seems like a better way of going about things; and perhaps we should go about it that way here. Strange, isn't it, how you can go galloping off in the wrong direction, and all of the enormous consequences that can follow from that, just by asking the wrong question. However, there is one little problem here. We don't know how to measure health, so how can we get it? Perhaps we should take just a moment or two to look at the Chinese definition of health. Their definition of health is understood in terms of the *ENERGY SYSTEM*, because the energy system is of a slightly different and 'higher' level than the flesh and blood and bones. The energy system functions as a 'control system' or 'blueprint' for the body. It lays down the basic framework. The hierarchical sequence of control and influence is as follows:

ENERGY/CHI > BLOOD > CELLS > TISSUES > ORGANS >
FUNCTIONS > RELATIONSHIPS > THE WHOLE

So if the basic level of your energy/control-system/blueprint is out of order then you are likely to get sick – your carburettor isn't working, the wiring is all wrong, the tyres are half flat, the steering is loose. The simple and blunt fact is that to get into the state of health you have to have your energy/chi working properly.

THE STATE OF HEALTH

So what is it, this mysterious state of energy-health? The state of correct functioning of your energy/control-system/blueprint can be described as when it works the way it is designed to, and how it is supposed to. This has four particular and specific characteristics that can be described as being when your energy is:

1. **Balanced** and
2. **Free-Flowing**, with
3. **The Right Quality**, and
4. **Good Volume.**

When you have these characteristics of Balance, Flow, Quality and Volume then you have the necessary foundation for the state of health.

The next obvious question is 'How do you measure it'? Well, subjectively, simply by the way you feel. Do you feel good, strong, bright, clear-headed, on top of things? Or do you have health problems or issues?

Acupuncturists and other Oriental doctors can technically measure this condition by feeling/palpating twelve separate 'pulses' on the wrists (see p.53), as well as by other indications such as a person's colour, the sound of their voice, the spirit in their eyes, their odour, mannerisms and emotions, and so on. However, the sum total is that somebody looks and 'feels' healthy. You know what it looks and feels like too – these are the people you feel attracted to and want to be around.

Acupuncturists, herbalists and other Oriental healers do something to you – use hair-thin needles, give you things to swallow, massage certain places in certain ways. But here, with Chi Kung, is something you can do yourself, by yourself, whenever you want, all day long if you wish. There's no reason not to do it.

By practising Chi Kung you will keep your energy fresh and strong throughout your life. This is the closely guarded and mysterious 'secret' of Chinese longevity. This is how to stay healthy for the rest of your life (and therefore not get ill) and how to minimize the ageing process. This is how to maintain your vitality and get into, and stay in, your best state-of-being. This is how to keep your body, soul, mind and spirit integrated, balanced and at peace.

COMMON CHARACTERISTICS OF ALL CHI KUNG

Chi Kung is used in different ways, at different levels, for a wide range of reasons and applications, which will be described in detail later. However, given the vast number and diversity of all the different traditions, styles and forms of Chi Kung there are some common characteristics that they all share together; there are certain things that they all have in common and ways in which they can all be categorized and understood. It may be that ultimately the individual and particular styles don't make much difference, it is the particular purpose that is important.

Following are some of the common characteristics and similarities of all Chi Kungs.

1. *Static and Dynamic*: There is a basic division into two major categories of Static and Dynamic Chi Kung. Static Chi Kung, which requires stillness, is called Nei-Dan. Dynamic Chi Kung, which involves movement, is called Wei-Dan. These are also respectively called the 'Internal Arts' and the 'External Arts'.
2. *Posture/Movement, Breathing and Mind*: All of the forms use combinations of these basic components.
3. *The Meridian System and the Acupoints*: All Chi Kung is based on the energy anatomy of the meridian system and the acupoints (described in detail in chapter 3) which are commonly familiar through acupuncture.
4. *The Three Tan T'ien/The Three Elixir Fields*: All forms focus on the three areas in the lower, middle and upper body (described later), which are major centres of energy.
5. *Organs and Tissues*: They all affect and cultivate the organs/viscera and the various tissues and functions of the body.

NEI-DAN AND WEI-DAN

Nei-Dan and Wei-Dan are the two fundamental categorizations of Chi Kung. These can be combined and integrated in many ways, but it is possible to know a great deal about one without knowing anything about the other. A novice may know only one or two aspects, a Master knows many. The basic characteristics are as follows:

Nei Dan / Static / Internal Chi Kung

Static, Nei-Dan Chi Kung is essentially performed internally. It includes all kinds of practices which are done without much external motion or movement. This can be considered meditation. These include such categories of practice as Relaxing Exercises, Breathing Exercises and Standing Exercises. The mind is fully conscious during these exercises. In the process of these practices the body functions change from energy consuming to energy restoring, and they thereby contribute to the body's ability to self-regulate, self-repair and self-regenerate. Specific Posture, Breathing and Mind methods are used to control and direct the chi in Static Chi Kung.

Posture

There are three basic variations of posture – standing, sitting and lying. Standing postures can be in a natural position, particular forms or in imagining doing certain activities – for instance imagining holding a large ball in front of you. Sitting postures can be done sitting in a chair, sitting crosslegged, or sitting leaning back against a support. Lying postures can be done lying on your back or on your side.

Postures place the body in particular geometric shapes which act to focus and 'drive' the body energy in a specific way.

Breathing

Breathing practice is a very precise and important aspect of Chi Kung, indeed Chi Kung is sometimes translated as 'breath control exercise'. Breathing brings into the body one of the three components of the body's energy – oxygen, the energy from heaven (which, along with food, the energy of earth, and the inherited energy of Yuan Chi in the kidneys, mixes to form the 'Essential Chi' which the body runs on).

The breath is controlled in four ways:

1. Relaxing (Quiescent) methods.
2. Abdominal breathing using various direct, reversed, continuous, stop-go and soft-hard methods.
3. Sending the breath very deep into the lower abdomen and also using 'opening' and 'closing' methods.
4. The use of certain words, as in The Six Healing Sounds whereby making specific sounds when breathing out discharges negative/pathogenic energy from each of the six major internal organs.

Mind
As with breathing there are various methods, techniques and reasons for mind focusing. By whatever mechanisms, currently unknown by ancient or modern science, the mind has the ability to direct the energy in the body. The five major methods of focusing the mind are:

1. Focusing on certain acupoints, such as the top of the head and the soles of the feet.
2. Focusing on beautiful and peaceful things such as the sky, trees, flowers, inspiring paintings and such like.
3. Focusing on a particular idea, person or memory.
4. Focusing on the meaning of words such as relaxation, tranquility, peace.
5. Focusing on particular lines or channels of energy.

Applying the Techniques
Using combinations of the techniques of Posture, Breathing and Mind there are a wide variety of ways to apply them.

- Relaxing exercises – which can involve relaxing all over, relaxing particular parts, relaxing one part after another, relaxing line by line. . .
- Quiescent Chi Kung – calming the mind.
- Breathing exercises using particular postures and patterns of breathing.
- Standing exercises which can be divided into basic, resting, and high, medium and low-level postures, each of which can be accompanied by many variations of arm and hand positions.
- Directing the chi along various meridians and channels and manipulating it for specifically desired purposes, for example up the central back channel and down the central front channel in the sequence known as 'The Microcosmic Orbit', or variations of possibilities along the central channel in the core of the body in processes called 'Inner Alchemy'.

Wei Dan / Dynamic / External Chi Kung

Dynamic, Wei-Dan Chi Kung is performed externally. It also uses breathing and mind, as in Nei-Dan, but instead of only static postures it involves movement. There are an uncountable number of these various exercises, sets, forms and sequences.

- Exercises that are good for waking oneself up in the morning, comparable to doing stretches.
- Classic forms, passed down through history, that have undergone innumerable permutations, variations and adaptations.
- Sets of exercises used for treating specific symptoms and conditions, which can be considered Medical Chi Kung.
- Sequences designed to cultivate physical fitness and strength, as in Hard Chi Kung and martial-arts training.
- Long-standing family secrets.
- Forms recently developed by experienced doctors and practitioners.
- Spiritually transforming procedures.

Some of these are easy to learn and do. Some are very hard and take a lot of time, patience and practice, if, indeed, you can find somebody willing to teach you. Some are so esoteric, refined and difficult that you would only be taught them in a monastic setting, and only after you had proven yourself worthy to receive such teachings.

Given this range and span of Dynamic Chi Kung it is obviously not possible to give a complete listing – not least because nobody will ever know exactly how many there are. However, below is a list of some of the most common and familiar ones.

- Exercises to prevent illness (Bao Jian Gong).
- Eight Pieces of Brocade / Eight Elegant Movements (Ba Duan Jing).
- Muscle and Tendon Training (Yi Jin Jing).
- Bone Marrow Washing (Xi Wue Jing).
- Shadow Boxing (Tai Chi Chi Kung).
- The Five Animal Frolics (Wu Qin Xi).
- Specific sets – Wild Goose, Flying Crane, Swimming Dragon. . .
- Natural Chi Kung (Lu Lu Dao Yin).
- Spontaneous Chi Kung.

Many of the moving sets are extraordinarily graceful and beautiful to watch, equal to the pleasure in watching dance. The fluidity and poise can leave you breathless, as one movement flows into another and images blend into each other, defying the mind to understand what the eyes see. At times it is as if you are literally watching the energy flow and it becomes a performance – and often it is indeed performed in front of an audience.

Like other skills, the more you do External Chi Kung the better you get. Learning a particular form embodies it in your being and it becomes part of you – part of the way you move and experience yourself. It is an investment in yourself.

CHI KUNG AND OTHER PRACTICES

There are specific characteristics that distinguish Chi Kung from other kinds of physical exercises such as aerobics, sports training, ballet and so on.

1. It uses a comprehensive knowledge of the body's chi and meridian system.
2. It is based upon the theories of Oriental anatomy and physiology.
3. It is done in an inward state of peace achieved through specific postures, breathing and mental focusing.
4. It requires calming the spirit and regulating chi in very particular ways.

IN SUMMARY

With so much potentially possible, how come everyone isn't doing Chi Kung every day? Well, in China a lot of people do. It is estimated that something in the order of 60,000,000 people in China now practise on a regular basis. That is more than the total population of Britain, and approximately one-quarter of the population of the United States.

As I hope has been made clear, there is a very wide range of forms, styles and purposes for Chi Kung – from keep-fit to spiritual evolution – and while there is often no common agreement between different teachers, traditions and authorities, there are characteristics which all Chi Kung forms share. Chi Kung uses terms, references and paradigms which are unfamiliar to the West, and for which we have no equivalent or adequate translation, so to understand Chi Kung you need to familiarize yourself with these terms and concepts.

When practised correctly Chi Kung makes you feel good and has many beneficial and desirable effects on your life, but remember, it has to be done right. It is advised that whenever possible you practise in a natural, calm, beautiful or inspiring location, preferably outdoors – you can draw the energy of the external environment into you and refresh and regenerate yourself. Learn it and make it part of your life. Once you know it, it is yours forever.

EXERCISE ONE

The Healing Smile

Learn to smile at your own internal organs, release tension and generate relaxation.

Purpose
A form of internal, static, quiescent Nei Dan. This is intended to relax and prepare your internal Yin organs, calm the mind and stabilize the metabolism.

The sequence
1. Find a comfortable position sitting on a chair with both feet flat on the floor, knees shoulder-width apart, and relax. Clasp your hands in front of you in your lap, with the right over the left, to seal-in your chi. This exercise can also be performed lying down – in which case let your clasped hands rest on your abdomen wherever comfortable.

2. Close your eyes. If thoughts occur in your mind gently let them go and bring your attention inside yourself. Pay attention to how you feel.

3. Find a thought, a memory, an image or a picture which causes you to smile – one of those warm smiles which gently softens the corners of your mouth.

4. Let the warm, soft, gentle energy of this smile grow and accumulate.

5. Your energy follows your mind. Using your mind bring this smiling

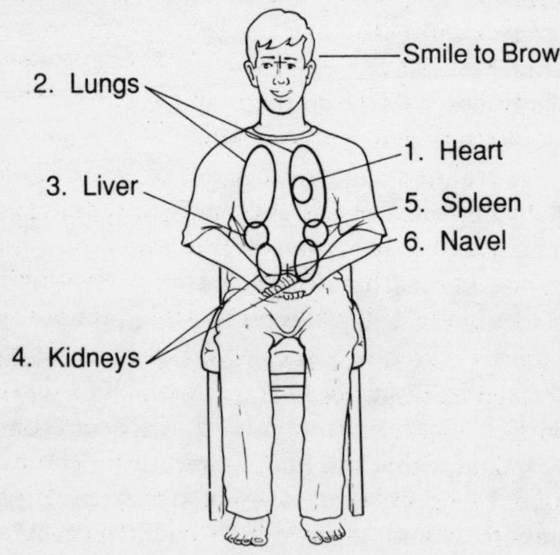

Fig. 2. The Healing Smile

energy to the point on your forehead between your eyes, and allow it to begin to increase at this point, like warm water slowly filling a deep bowl.

6. Connect the tip of your tongue with the roof of the palate in your mouth, just behind the top of your teeth. This lets the energy flow through your tongue and throat into your torso. Using your mind you are going to direct and send your energy into your heart, lungs, liver, kidneys and spleen, and then gather it at your navel.

If you do not know the general anatomy and location of each organ, then look it up in a textbook or just trust your own internal knowledge (your unconscious mind knows about your internal anatomy because it is all you). If you do not have a particular organ, for medical reasons, then smile into the general area, because the energy channel/meridian runs there and feeds into all of the related functions.

In each organ you can hold the healing energy of your smile as long as you wish, or for the count of a certain number of breaths, or until you feel it overflow – the amount of time depends on you. This is indicated by the instructions 'Hold your chi there'.

7. Directing the energy with your mind, send this warm, smiling, loving energy to your heart. All day long and every day your heart is working for you. This is an opportunity to 'thank' your heart and to give it your gentle love and care. Let your heart fill with smiling energy. Hold it there as long as you wish, or feel the need to, or until you feel it overflow.

8. Now send your smiling energy to your lungs. All day long and every day your lungs are working to bring fresh clear energy into you, and to send out the old stale energy you have used. This is an opportunity to 'thank' and appreciate your lungs and to send them your best love and care. Let your lungs fill with smiling energy. Hold your chi there.

9. Now send your warm, smiling, healing energy to your liver. Your liver is situated below your rib cage on your right side and is the largest organ in your body. All day long and every day your liver works for you. This is an opportunity to 'thank' your liver for everything it does. Let your liver fill with smiling, loving energy. Hold your chi there.

10. Now, using your mind send your energy to your kidneys. Your kidneys are located half-way between the bottom of your rib cage and the top of your pelvis, level with your waist. They are about the size of clenched fists and are either side of the spine, about one-third in from your back. All day long and every day your kidneys work for you. Take this opportunity to smile at your kidneys and appreciate and 'thank' them. Hold your chi there.

11. Now, send your warm, gentle, loving chi to your spleen. Your spleen is on the left side of the body, just below the rib cage, opposite your liver. All day long and every day your spleen works for you. Smile at your spleen and 'thank' it. Hold your chi there.

12. Now, finally, use your mind to send your chi to your navel. When it is at your navel, let go of your smile from the corners of your mouth, so that your mouth is relaxed and neutral, and bring your warm current of smiling energy through one organ after the other – your heart, lungs, liver, kidneys and spleen – slowly winding it in until it all finally comes to rest in your navel.

13. If you are a man place the centre of your left palm over your navel, then cover it with the centre of your right palm. If you are a woman, place your right palm over your navel and cover it with your left. Stay in this position and feel the warm energy in your navel. This is your chi. It is now in your Centre. Concentrate on feeling and experiencing it there.

14. Pay attention to how you now feel, and find a word, phrase, image or symbol to describe it. Remember this; it is your personal internal 'key' to your own chi. Just thinking of this 'key' can re-activate some of the relaxation you have experienced through this exercise – which can help as preparation in future practice, or as a refresher in the midst of your busy everyday life.

15. Relax your hands and let them take any comfortable position, and slowly open your eyes, one eyelash after the other, and return back to the outside.

You have now smiled at your main internal organs. We are all accustomed to giving our love to the special people in our life – this simple process is a way to send your own warm, gentle, loving energy to yourself. It is a simple practical way of taking care of, and loving, yourself. It releases tension and stress and generates deep relaxation. There are many other effects from doing this procedure – it calms your emotions, refreshes your sense organs and benefits the various tissues, amongst other benefits. It also makes you feel good.

Learn it and you can use it whenever you need to, or whenever you wish. It is one of the kindest things you can do for yourself. Smile, please!

2

The Story of Chi Kung

BEFORE CONTINUING FURTHER into the details of Chi Kung it is perhaps best to step back and look at it from the right historical and cultural perspective, otherwise taken out of context it may just seem strange and peculiar. In order to avoid a Western cultural myopia and bias in describing something so foreign and unfamiliar, we need to start with a short conducted tour of the history of China, Taoism and Chi Kung.

THE HISTORY OF CHINA

What we know as China, the country with its borders and the people who live there that we call the Chinese, are all named after one person, much the same way that America and Americans are named after an Italian – Amerigo Vespucci. Prior to 221 BC China was divided into many separate areas and ruled by different dynasties. There is reported to have been a legendary kingdom called Hsia as far back as 2,000 BC. From approximately 1,000 BC to 221 BC there was a feudal age, which ended with 250 years of the so-called Warring States period.

In 246 BC, a young man named Chao Cheng ascended to the throne of one of the small states. By 221 BC he had progressively conquered all of the other states and created one country. He used his family name along with the name of one of the great legendary Emperors, and called himself Chhin Shih Huang Ti, The First Emperor of Chhin. He unified the country for the first time, disbanded the ancient feudalist system, created a common civil code and established one written language. His rule was draconian.

He only ruled for fourteen years, and eventually disintegrated in spiritual occult chaos – he is said to have died in battle with the Dragon King – but his influence was so great that his family name of Chhin became the basis for the name of the land and its people – China and the Chinese.

One major conditioning fact about Chinese history is the nature of the Chinese written language. It is pictographic, based upon what the images and symbols look like. In the West the foundation of our language is phonetic, based upon how it sounds. We speak and sound differently from place to place, and country to country, with dialects and pronunciations which change from time to time, therefore separate languages have developed. In China the written language stayed the same, so somebody in one end of the country could perfectly understand the writing of someone at the other end of the country, although they may have no idea of what the other person was saying if they tried to speak directly to each other. This common written language allowed the spread of information and communication.

Another very significant fact was the invention of paper (1,200 years before the West) and the development of printing (600 years before the West). People wrote great classics of thought and intellectual investigation and the books were passed down from generation to generation in an uninterrupted continuation. Along the way other people wrote commentaries on those books (sometimes hundreds of years later), then others wrote commentaries on the commentaries, so that there has been a continuous tradition. There were, as always, the occasional frenzies of book burnings by repressive emperors, but the major classics survived.

During this time, comparable to the Golden Age of ancient Greece, some of the most profound and enlightened thinkers of China's history appeared, who determined and still underlie and influence its culture – Lao Tzu, Chuang Tzu, Lieh Tzu, K'ung Fu-tzu (Confucius) amongst others. These people were not all related – Tzu simply means Master. Some of the most important and influential books were written – *The I Ching* (*The Book of Changes*, written around 1,000 BC, and considered to be the oldest extant book), *The Nei Ching* (*The Classic of Internal Medicine*), *The Tao Te Ching* (*The Book of The Way and its Virtue*). For many of these classics there are no known authors and no specific time of writing or compilation – their origins are lost in legend and pre-history.

After the death of the first emperor the history of China progressed in a yo-yo like fashion over the next thousand years or so, in what might be considered a Yin/Yang polarity. First it would be unified, then it would break apart into different feudal states, only to be unified again by some determined emperor. After the First Unification of Chhin there were a number of small dynasties which ended with the First Partition from 221 BC to AD 265. This was followed by the Second Unification from 265 to 479 and then the Second Partition from 479 to 581, followed by the Third Unification from 581 to 906, and the Third Partition from 907 to 1227. For the last thousand years or so China has been unified, although under different dynasties.

For a fascinating and comprehensive account of all of this to-ing and fro-ing, and a sense of the texture of what life was like in this enormous country during these ages, I refer you to the magnificent opus of the English scholar Professor Joseph Needham – *Science and Civilization in China.*

Having been insulated from outside influences for all of its history, at the end of the last century China was opened up to the Western world, with its science and technology, and this exposure greatly influenced it in its attempts to modernize. Following World War II the Communists gained power, and have since established a state where information and education is strictly controlled by the government.

One very important fact, the significance of which it may be difficult for us to fully grasp, is that in mainland China there has never been a democracy. In their whole history the Chinese have never voted! It is also important to recognize that the influence of Chinese culture extends beyond the borders of the mainland, and that much of the traditional culture, and Chi Kung practice, are carried on as they always have been in Hong Kong, Taiwan and other areas. Outside of the mainland all of the traditional varieties and styles of Chi Kung flourish.

Possibly the most important aspect of the difference between the way that we in the West look at the world and experience ourselves in it, and how the Chinese look at the world, is that their view of life is organized around and based upon the understanding of energy, while ours is based upon the mastery of material objects. It is the contrast between a reductionist mechanical model and a spiritual energetic model. There is a very important difference between East and West in the understanding of just what a human being is! This difference is the reason that we have no Western equivalent to Chi Kung. To appreciate this more we need to look at the history of Taoism.

THE HISTORY OF TAOISM

Taoism is the major tradition at the root of Chi Kung. In China, as in every other major civilization, there was a wide range of religious, spiritual and political movements and over the course of history different schools grew, developed, flourished and declined. There were the Confucians, the Naturalists, the Buddhists, the Mohists, the Logicians, the Legalists and others, each at various times rising to prominence and influence, then declining. Although there are forms of Buddhist, Confucian and Tibetan Chi Kung, by far the most influential and relevant group were the Taoists.

Taoism is a natural philosophy. It is based upon observation and alignment with the natural and organic order of things – from planetary movements and the progression of the seasons, to our feelings and mental functions. The Taoists can be thought of as early scientists. They observed nature, understood its ways and aspired to act in accord with it. Today, in China, Taoism is still very much alive. This reflects on its importance and significance – it is ever resilient and impossible to repress, adapting to the conditions and circumstances of the times.

Lao Tzu and The Tao Te Ching

Taoism is a mix of many elements. The name is taken from the book *The Tao Te Ching* which is attributed to Lao Tzu and was supposedly written in the fifth century BC. It can be translated as 'The Book of the Way of Virtue'. It is said that Lao Tzu wrote the book after giving up public office and before 'riding off into the sunset on his Ox'; although we could interpret this allegorically as meaning before he died. There is, indeed, no solid evidence of the existence of Lao Tzu as a real person. However, some 300 years after he was considered to have died the name 'Taoism' was first used by followers of the writings. If Lao Tzu did exist he was one of those very evolved people who deeply understood the nature of things –

such a person is called a 'sage' in China. Reportedly his real name was Li Erh, as Lao Tzu simply means Old Master. Lao Tzu never defined the Tao. The Tao is immanent and transcendent. It is beyond the ability of language to describe it. It is a state of consciousness and an attitude towards life and living.

Whether Lao Tzu wrote the book, or whether various statements and phrases were simply attributed to him over the course of a few hundred years, will never be known. It is a collection of thoughts and teachings. It uses paradox to force us to rethink. It contains pieces of information, like proverbs, strung together without any real connection or meaning between them – a collection of insights and wisdom reflective of a particular attitude to life. The text explores the issues of knowledge, of time, of origin, of language and meaning, of the physical and non-physical and of 'The Way'.

Chuang Tzu and Lieh Tzu

Two other major figures of Taoism were Chuang Tzu and Lieh Tzu. Chuang Tzu lived in the reign of King Hui and King Hsuan of Ch'i during the Warring States period, 370–301 BC. He saw the sage as a recluse who rejected power, authority and position as illusion and dangerous. He was concerned with freeing the mind from conventional ideas and patterns of behaviour, to break with convention and see deeper into the nature of things. For him, this way leads to freedom.

This attitude to freedom expressed by Chuang Tzu was exemplified by an extraordinary bunch of drunken poets of this period known as The Seven Sages of the Bamboo Grove, who defied convention and common standards and used humour and outrage to illuminate their view of life, much as groups of poets and artists have always done. Given the strict Confucian puritanism of the time this may have been like having the notorious 1950s Beat Poets group of Jack Kerouac, Allen Ginsberg, Gregory Corso et al at the court of Queen Victoria!

Lieh Tzu was revered by Chuang Tzu as a sage. He was reputedly a recluse, who lived in the wilds removed from the world. The book which bears his name, from the second and third centuries BC, is a collection of stories, jokes, tales, practical tricks, legends, reflection and thoughtful quotes. To Lieh Tzu, the Tao is understood as the origin and purpose of life, it is immanent and all pervading, therefore providing unity and the perfection of all life through fusion with it. His book has been used as a manual for immortality training, whereby those who wish to learn must start humbly and progress stage by stage – not by questions but by patient observation, reflection and development. Lieh Tzu uses stories and teachings to help people find The Way.

While there were many other Taoist teachers, some of the essential characteristics of Taoism can be summarized as:

1. They believed in a basic political collectivism, a concern with social welfare and socialism.
2. There was a pre-occupation with religious mysticism.
3. Much emphasis was placed on training of the individual for immortality.
4. The foundation of scientific attitude was established – with a concern for observing nature. The Taoists were early scientists.

Basic principles

There are basic principles of Taoism which underlie its attitude to life. There is the principle of Wu-Wei, perhaps best described as non-action or non-interference. Wu-Wei is the art of being in such harmony with the Tao that everything happens as it should, of its own accord. We have all had the experience of doing something exactly right, so that it all went perfectly. This is Wu-Wei.

Another principle is that of change. Change is the essence of The Way. We all know everything changes, but there are underlying principles for this change, which are not always obvious. The laws of the interactions of Yin and Yang (see p.58) describe the nature of such change – for example Yin changes into Yang and Yang changes into Yin. The principles of change are exemplified in the great classic of Chinese thought, *The I Ching: The Book of Changes* – which in many ways is the Taoist's bible.

Other basic principles are those of Transformation, Relativity, Yieldingness and the Feminine Principle which in total have been described as 'The Water Way'. Water is a primary symbol for Taoists – it flows on, it fills all of the open spaces, it is unstoppable, it always finds the easiest course. Taoists were concerned with understanding the order of nature, the natural order of things, and aligning themselves with it.

The Taoists also believed in magic, the existence of other realms of nature not perceivable by ordinary consciousness. There was a belief in the notion of the immortal, the Hsien, the idea of a perfected person who never dies, lives on nothing but air and travels through the sky at will. Emperors searched for the Elixir of Life and Immortality. This is reflective of the world view of the Shamans, where other levels of reality interact with, and influence, our own. The Shaman believes in two worlds – the material world and the spirit world – and that they themselves are the bridge between heaven and earth. The belief in a Magician Shaman is not specific to China but is common to many cultures.

To the Taoists, the Tao is the primary ground of everything. This basic credo is reflected in Chapter 42 of the *Tao Te Ching*:

> The Tao is the origin of the One,
> The One created the two,
> The two formed the three.
> From the three came forth all life.

From Tao comes origin; Yin and Yang; heaven, earth and man; and thus all forms of existence.

'Pure' Taoism and Folk Taoism

There was never a pure Taoism. Folk Taoism did not degenerate from pure Taoism, because there was never a pure Taoism to begin with. Taoism was named 300 years after Lao Tzu, and by this time it had incorporated much of the folk beliefs and religion of the ordinary people. Folk Taoism was the religion and faith of the ordinary people, and various schools and traditions with their own temples and priests developed over the years. In Folk Taoism there are legendary, saint-like figures – The Eight Immortals – embodying what we might now describe as the basic archetypes of human nature. There was a Taoist 'Pope'. There was a Taoist Hell. There is a Taoist Canon, the collection of essential scriptures on every aspect of life. There were folk stories and tales – such as 'Seven Taoist Masters', 'Journey To The West', 'Romance Of The Three Kingdoms' – which the ordinary people knew by heart like we know fairy stories and legends.

But above all else there was one thing that all Taoists aspired to, a goal to achieve and be measured by, and this was 'To Attain

The Tao' – to achieve the state of being, in which one understood, embodied and lived in the Tao.

THE HISTORY OF CHI KUNG

The practice of Chi Kung goes back before recorded history; it is stated that historically there were over a hundred books written. One of the earliest references related to a tribe called Tao Tang. A statement from 'The Spring and Autumn Annals' by Master Lu, a history book written around 230 BC, stated that, 'A long, long time ago dancing was used to aid the flow of chi and blood.' During a period of intense flooding, there was a lot of excessive dampness which caused the stasis of body fluids and clogging dampness. This resulted in rheumatism and contractions of tendons and muscles due to stagnation of chi and blood, and other related problems. Dance exercises were developed to relieve stagnation, and these gradually developed into physical and breathing therapies.

The *Yellow Emperor's Classic of Internal Medicine/Huang Ti Nei Ching* is the earliest extant medical text, written during the Warring States period, which ended in 221 BC. The Nei Ching systematically expounded Chi Kung principles, training methods and effects of practice. It devotes many chapters to detailing the origin, application, clarification and theory of Chi Kung. These include ridding the mind of worries, controlling and concentrating thought, breathing exercises, muscle toning, swallowing saliva to preserve it, bringing into play the body's physiological forces and stimulating circulation. An entry on breathing techniques states: 'When one is completely at ease, free of desire and ambition, one will get the genuine energy in order and one's mind concentrated. How then can disease invade one's being?' Also 'Exhale and inhale essence Qi, concentrate the spirit to keep a sound mind, the muscles and flesh unite as one.' In the book Chi Kung is considered an important measure for treating disease and protecting health, and the appropriate exercise method is recorded.

Lao Tzu suggested methods of health preservation by regulating respiration and by 'blowing and puffing'. Chuang Tzu said: 'Inhaling and exhaling helps to rid one of the stale and take in the fresh. Moving as a bear and stretching as a bird can result in longevity.' He also stated 'The men of old breathed clear down to their heels' which was not a figure of speech, but confirmed that a breathing method for chi circulation was being used by some Taoists at that time.

Instructions for Chi Kung were found on a historical relic known as the 'Jade Pendant Inscriptions of Chi Direction' from 380 BC. This recorded the training method and theory. The inscription was engraved on a twelve-sided cylinder, containing forty-five characters on it which state:

> To make chi flow freely one must be smooth and steady. In this way chi can be preserved and extended deeply throughout the body. Flowing downward it is consolidated. This stimulates chi proliferation which will carry it up to the sky [to the head]. The base of the sky is above, the foundation of the earth extends into the depths. If you abide by this principle you will lead a long life; otherwise you will die.

Or, in another translation

> In promoting and conducting Chi, depth promises storage, storage promises extension, extension promises descent, descent promises stability, stability promises solidity, solidity promises germination, germination promises growth, growth promises retreat, retreat leads to heaven. Heavenly chi functions from above, earthly chi functions from below. Conformity to this leads to life, while adverseness to this leads to death.

Here not only the training process of the method called 'the Microcosmic Orbit/the Small Heavenly Circuit' is clearly explained, but the health-preserving principles of Chi Kung are also expounded.

The Silk Roll was a recent major discovery. During excavations in 1973 a silk roll/book was unearthed from the early western Han Dynasty (206 BC – 8 AD). It contained two chapters on Chi Kung:

1. A treatise entitled 'Nutrition from the air instead of food' – which describes diseases treated with breathing and chi direction, and methods of practice.

2. An atlas of Dao Yin – forty-four coloured drawings illustrating movements of the body with captions under the drawings, including:

(a) Drawings with diseases or symptoms on pain in the knee, arthritis, deafness and irritability.
(b) Various animal figures imitating the bear, monkey, wolf, crane, dragon and hawk – to limber up joints.
(c) Drawings illustrating combined movements of joints and breathing.

(d) Drawings characterized by the combination of motion and tranquillity – including direction of chi by the combination of thought, respiration, joint movements and speaking.

The complexity and comprehensiveness of this document establishes that Chi Kung was well developed before the Han Dynasty and that China already used a form of illustration to teach Chi Kung by this period.

THE CLASSIC FORMS OF CHI KUNG

Writings about Chi Kung have appeared throughout Chinese history. The following are some of the origins of the major forms.

The Five Animal Frolics

Hua To, the Leonardo Da Vinci of Chinese medicine, created The Five Animal Frolics (Wu Qin Xi) in the second century AD, the earliest systematic method of Daoyin for physical training. These exercises mimic the movements and gestures of the tiger, the deer, the bear, the monkey and the bird (crane). They were performed in order to attain the goal of 'free circulation of blood and prevention of disease occurrence'. There are many, many variations of Wu Qin Xi developed by different teachers and families over the generations, and now widely practised throughout the world.

The Muscle and Tendon Changing Classic and The Bone Marrow Washing Classic

During the Liang dynasty (AD 502–557) the Emperor invited a Buddhist monk named Da Mo, who was once an Indian prince, to preach Buddhism in China. After the Emperor decided he did not like what Da Mo had to say, the monk retired to the Shaolin Temple. When he arrived there he saw that the monks were sickly and weak, so he shut himself up for nine years to consider the problem. As a result he created two books *Muscle and Tendon Changing Classic/Yi Jin Jing* and *Bone Marrow Washing Classic/Xi Xue Jing*. These taught the priests how to change their physical bodies from weak to strong and thereby develop their health.

The Marrow Washing Classic taught them how to use chi to clean the bone marrow and strengthen the blood and immune system, as well as how to energize the brain and attain enlightenment. The training was integrated into martial arts forms and increased the effectiveness of the techniques, for which the Shaolin Temple has become famous.

The Six Healing Sounds

Sun Si Miao of the Tang Dynasty, AD 581–682, wrote *Documents of Yimen*, which contains a 'Song of Hygiene' that says 'Breathing exercises make the eyesight clear in spring, strengthen the heart in summer, reinforce the lungs in autumn and tone-up the kidneys in winter. Constant breathing exercises expel evil fever and improve digestive functioning.' He described a method called The Six Healing Sounds, of which there are now many variations, which uses sound and posture to cleanse negative/impure energy from the body.

Tai Chi Chuan

Not long after the Shaolin Temple started to use Chi Kung training in the Song Dynasty it is believed that Chang San-Feng created the form known as Tai Chi Chuan. This follows a different approach to Shaolin in its use of Chi Kung – it integrates Nei Dan Chi Kung (Internal Elixir) with movement, while Shaolin emphasizes Wei Dan Chi Kung (External Elixir).

The Eight Pieces of Brocade

During the Southern Song Dynasty (AD 1127–1279) Marshal Yeuh Fei was credited with creating several internal Chi Kung exercises and martial arts. It is considered that he created 'The Eight Pieces of Brocade', a series/set of exercises that address the whole body, in order to maintain his soldiers' health. Additionally he is said to have developed the internal martial arts style known as Hsing Yi.

Spontaneous Chi Kung

Undirected spontaneous movements are inherent in the human condition, and are part of the Chi Kung legacy. Allowing whatever movement wants to happen – stretching, twisting, shaking, bending, jumping – is an expression of energy in the body. They allow the body to move in whatever direction it wants to, and can let it find its own equilibrium. In spontaneous Chi Kung these are seen as manifestations of the energy of the heart, spleen, lungs, kidneys and liver, and are traditionally described respectively as related to the animal types of the bird, monkey, tiger, bear and deer. A familiar recent comparison in the West to spontaneous Chi Kung is the field known as Bioenergetics; another is Dynamic Meditation.

Lulu Daoyin

This is a form of Chi Kung to music, without any fixed style or specific set of movements. It is performed in response to music, and the music moves the body in whatever way it wants. Anybody can do it, and it quickly stimulates and induces a strong sensation of energy/chi. Different kinds and qualities of music can be used for different purposes and results – to stimulate, to calm, to solidify, to excite. This form may be very familiar to modern Westerners – in Discos and Rock'n'Roll. Lulu Daoyin may be one of the oldest forms of Chi Kung. It might best be described as Natural Dance.

MEDICAL CHI KUNG

Chinese medical doctors have understood the importance of Chi Kung to maintaining health. The following are some of the most renowned and cherished of these.

Fig. 3. Rock'n'Roll – Chi Kung?

Zhang Zhong Jing was an outstanding physician of the Han Dynasty who wrote *Treatise on Febrile and Miscellaneous Diseases* and *Synopsis of Prescriptions of the Golden Chamber* (*Jin Kui Yao Lue*). In one section he stated 'As soon as the limbs feel heavy and sluggish, resort to such treatments as Daoyin, tu na (expiration and inspiration), acupuncture and massage by rubbing with ointment so as to allow the orifices to close up.'

Ge Hong held that the methods of Daoyin should be diversified. In his book *Bao Puzi's Inner Treaties* he stated 'Flexibility or stretching, bending or up-facing, walking or lying, leaning or standing, pacing or strolling, chanting or breathing are all methods of Daoyin.' He believed that the function of Chi Kung is 'to cure diseases not yet contracted and dredge discordant Qi. Once it gets working, Qi will flow unimpeded everywhere.' He also commented on applying exhalation and inhalation, expiration and inspiration to 'conducting Qi', which can 'keep good health internally and eliminate pathogenic factors externally'.

Zhu Xi of the Song Dynasty, AD 1130–1200, wrote *Maxim for Breathing Exercises*. In it he says: 'Concentrate the mind on the tip of your nose. Relax all parts of your body. Exhale at the end of extreme quietness just like fish swimming in the spring, then inhale like a hibernating worm.' This visually depicts the comfortable sensation after meditation in breathing exercises.

Li Shi Zhen of the Ming Dynasty, 1518–1593 AD, recorded in his book *A Study on the Eight Extra Channels*: 'The inner scene and channels can be perceived clean and clear only by those who can see inwards', also 'Changes in the channels and collaterals can be perceived by noting the physiological reactions during Quiescent Chi Kung.' He pointed out in his *Guidebook to Acupuncture and Moxibustion* that those who learn acupuncture and moxibustion should practise still-sitting exercises first, so that 'in the human body the circulation of Chi and blood in the channels and the opening and closing of the functional activities of Chi can have a reliable foundation'.

To bring us up to the contemporary era: in the first half of this century in mainland China, traditional medicine was banned in the rush to modernization and emulation of the West. After Mao Tse Tung came to power in the 1940s he recognized the enormous value of traditional knowledge, and instructed officials to research 'The Storehouse of Treasures'. In the early 1950s, research of Chi Kung was started, but this was abandoned during the ten year Cultural Revolution from 1966 to 1976, when Chi Kung and other practices were again outlawed. From the late 1970s onward the government has conducted research on the effects of Chi Kung, as it once again re-emerged amongst the common people and Chi Kung Masters began demonstrating undeniable abilities and powers, many of which involved remarkable acts of medical healing. This has been most startlingly seen in scientifically documented cures of cancer.

There is a major concern on the part of the authorities in the People's Republic with understanding its function, and developing some form of measurement in order to grade and certify different levels of Masters. Some people have been found guilty of fraudulently misrepresenting Chi Kung for the own personal financial advantage – 'profiteers', as they are officially called – and have been jailed. Today in China many hospitals and clinics now provide treatments in Chi Kung healing, which is applied in clinical settings – by practitioners in white coats.

However, apart from its applications in healing, Chi Kung also represents the re-emergence of the spiritual roots of Taoism amongst the ordinary people, which challenges the government's authority. Whereas ten years ago anybody could set up a class in a public park and teach whoever turned up, these teachers now have to register in advance with the local appropriate supervisory department. However, the essential nature of Taoism is that it follows the flow of least resistance, which is how it has survived through 2,000 years and is still vital today, and Chi Kung can be passed on in small private groups, so it is not altogether proving easy to supervise or control.

CHI KUNG IN THE WEST TODAY – CROSS-CULTURAL TRANSLATION

There are a number of areas of confusion and problems regarding the differences in attitude between East and West, which, for the sake of clarity, need to be addressed at this stage. One major issue that has plagued other aspects of Oriental arts which are already established in the West – acupuncture and martial arts – is the translation of attitudes and concepts.

In the field of acupuncture, for instance, there has been enormous confusion and conflict for the past twenty-five years about the relative and respective roles and positions of the various styles and traditions of acupuncture. This is relevant to us because acupuncture is now so widespread and firmly established in the West. From the beginning there have been many different styles of acupuncture. Western students that went over to China and the East in the 1950s learned a particular style from a particular teacher, other people went to other teachers, or other Eastern countries, and learned differently. Orientals came to the West and brought a particular tradition with them. This was greatly complicated by the fact that there was a very definite shift in the texture and fabric of acupuncture on the mainland after the Communist revolution in 1947. Subsequently anything that has come out as a formal or official statement since then has to be considered, and borne in mind, as being filtered through the current government. The current books and manuals published on acupuncture by the various formal institutions in China have to be understood as representing 'Post-Communist Revolution Acupuncture' and not the Classical Taoist tradition.

For instance, the body of knowledge and inherent attitude that is the predominant style practised in the USA, and which forms the basis of the National Acupuncture examination (and therefore the basis for licensing in many states) is known as Traditional Chinese Medicine (TCM), with everything that implies. However, it has recently come to light that the term TCM, and the knowledge and the approach that it incorporates, was in fact invented in the 1950s. The story appears to be that when Chairman Mao Tse Tung recognized China's 'Storehouse of Treasures' and proclaimed that they should be shared with the world, the Chinese Communist government officials decided that one of the most important priorities was to establish Chinese medicine, and specifically acupuncture because it is unique in World Medicine, and have it accepted by the World Health Organization (WHO).

They set about compiling the body of knowledge based on what they thought would fit into the picture of dialectical materialism/ communism and be acceptable to the WHO. They therefore left out, ignored, lost or otherwise did not include anything that had any reference to the non-physical, the spiritual or the old traditions, including Taoism. They denied their own enormous spiritual heritage. This has caused tremendous confusion in the field of acupuncture, which is only now beginning to be recognized. Hopefully, this can be avoided in Chi Kung.

A similar attitude prevails in the field of martial arts, as anybody who has trained in one particular style can attest. The level of competitiveness and intensity of rivalry between different styles and teachers is at times beyond belief. The energy that can go into statements disclaiming another teacher and another style has a charge similar to hostile sectarian warfare which comes out of a long history of feudalism. We could make a comparison to competing football teams or local government departments in present Western society.

That this basic misrepresentation and misunderstanding of the whole field and scope of a body of knowledge can happen to Chi Kung, is, I believe, a very valid and important concern.

- Just because a particular teacher publishes a book, or collection of books, does not mean that it represents the whole story.
- Just because something comes out of present day China as an officially approved state manual, does not necessarily mean that it is comprehensive.
- Just because an author is Chinese does not mean that they are unbiased or know the complete picture.

It would be useful to help forestall the kind of misunderstanding and conflict which has eaten at the soul of acupuncture and martial arts in the West over the last twenty-five years, and caused tremendous confusion for a whole generation.

I most sincerely hope that this text may make a contribution to Chi Kung as it enters the West – by outlining the shape of the board, describing the pieces on it and understanding how they each move.

All of the remarkable effects and changes of Chi Kung happen through very exact energetic structures and functions in the body, and take place according to invariable rules and principles. These structures are the meridian system, with its specific anatomy and physiology, and the various laws of Chinese philosophy and medicine. For any further practical understanding of Chi Kung it is now necessary to explain these systems and principles in some working detail.

EXERCISE TWO

The Energy Shower

Draw external chi into you, and use it to clean out negative energy and refresh you.

Purpose

An external, dynamic, Wei Dan form. This is a preparatory exercise to cleanse negative energy from the major front, middle and back meridians, to prepare the meridians for further practice and to bring fresh chi from the outside into you.

The sequence

A) Clearing the Front Channel

1. Stand with feet parallel and flat on the floor, shoulder-width apart, knees soft, shoulders relaxed and arms hanging naturally down by your sides. Your mind should be clear, and you should be breathing slowly and evenly. If necessary or desired this exercise can be performed sitting, in which case it is preferable to sit upright on the edge of a chair. Don't slump, as it tends to inhibit or block your chi.

2. Slowly raise your arms out to the sides, bringing them upwards until they are directly above your head, elbows slightly bent. Inhale as your

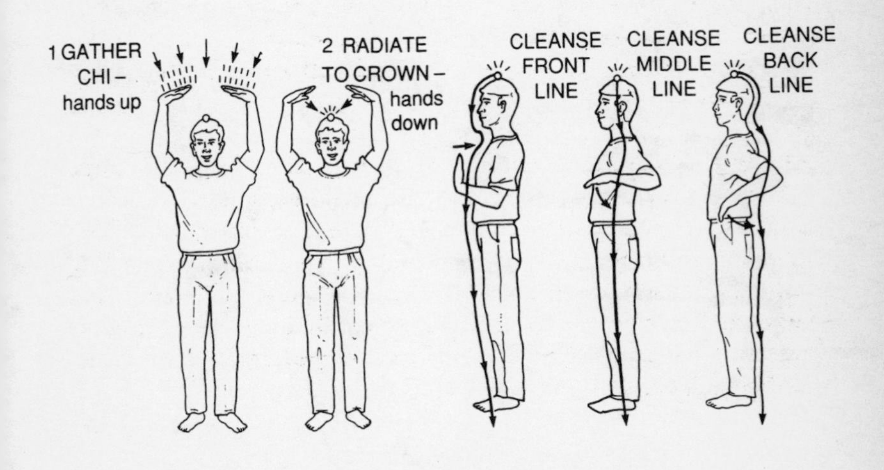

Fig. 4. The Energy Shower

arms come up. Bend your head back so that your eyes are looking up between your hands. Flex your wrists so that the flat palms are facing towards the sky. Exhale.

3. As you breathe in again draw the fresh chi of the sunlight/ moonlight/heavens (from above the clouds if there are any) to gather this chi in your palms. Let your palms fill with this fresh, clean energy, as if they were sponges soaking up heavenly chi. Feel it accumulate. When you breathe out don't let any of this chi disperse, but just hold the energy in your palms using your mind and will. Let your feet be flat and grounded on the earth/floor. In this position you are standing between heaven and earth.

The energy in your palms can be directed outside you, like the beam of a flashlight. In this exercise you will use this energy beam, through the way that you angle and point your palms and also by directing it with your mind, to clean negative energy out of your system.

4. Face forward so that the top of your head is upright and level. Your eyes may be open, closed or half-way between – whichever is most comfortable, effective or desirable for you. Slowly turn your palms over so that they are facing downwards to the top of your head. Angle your palms so that their energy beams are directed to the point on the very top of your crown. This is the Bai Hui point / The Meeting Of The Hundred – one of the major Chi Kung points. Using your mind and will, send and radiate the energy that you have gathered in your palms to this point on the top of your head.

5. Hold this position for a moment. Feel the chi. Now, as you sl – o – w – ly exhale through your mouth, bring your hands and palms down in front of your body, so that your palms are facing down towards the floor and the tips of the fingers of each hand are facing each other 3 to 6 inches (7.5 to 15 cm) apart – as if they were resting on top of a balloon and slowly pushing it down in front of you. See them as sweeping down the front energy channel of your body (this is the Conception Meridian), from the top of your head down the centre-front, all the way down to the perineum (the lowest point of your torso between your legs). Then, having reached the lowest point that your hands go so that they are hanging by your sides naturally, just using your mind only, continue on down the front of your legs through and out of the soles of your feet.

6. When you reach the soles of your feet continue on down with your mind, so that you push any negative chi out 3 feet (90 cm) below you. This is outside of your personal energy field.

Although this procedure may seem long and complex at first, after a small amount of practice it is easily possible to do it during one slow exhalation.

(If you are in a building where there are other floors, and people, below you, do not be concerned – once the negative chi is outside of your own individual field it will just disperse harmlessly into the atmosphere, like a drop of water in an ocean.)

7. Repeat this procedure at least twice more, for a minimum of three times.

B) Clearing the Middle Channel

8. Repeat 1, 2, 3 and 4 above. These are the preparatory movements and you end up with your palms above your head, loaded with heavenly chi and radiating down to your crown point.

9. Hold this position for a moment. Now, as you Sl – o – w – ly exhale, again bring your hands and palms down facing towards the floor, but this time down your sides, with fingers pointing forward. Imagine that you are pushing down a bigger balloon than before. See the energy in your palms as sweeping down through the central core of your body, in the middle of your body in front of the spine, from the top of your head to your perineum (this is called the Thrusting Channel/Meridian). See the energy in your palms dragging out and cleaning any negative chi from this central core. When you have reached the bottom of your torso and the lowest point of your hands, continue on down using your mind alone through the central core of your legs, to come out through the soles of your feet.

10. After reaching the soles of your feet continue on down with your mind, until you push any negative chi out 3 feet (90 cm) below you, outside of the edge of your energy field. Let your hands, body and mind relax.

11. Repeat this procedure at least two more times.

C) Clearing the Back Channel

12. Repeat 1, 2, 3 and 4 above. These preparatory movements end again with your palms above your head, loaded with clean, fresh heavenly chi and radiating down to your crown point.

13. Hold this position for a moment and 'feel' it. Let it soak into you. Breath in and out slowly and savour the sensation.

14. Sl – o – w – ly breathe out, and as you do let your hands descend again, with your palms facing down towards the floor, but this time with your shoulders as wide, back and open as possible. As you bring your hands down they are now on either side of your head and body, but

this time with the tips of your fingers pointing towards each other. Your hands sweep down the sides of your body. As you do this, angle your palms and use your mind to direct the energy beam down the energy line on the back of your head and then down the centre of your back (this is the Governor Meridian). Slowly bring them down as if you are sweeping and cleaning any negative chi out of the channel along the mid-line of your back. Run this down the central back line to the perineum, then using your mind-concentration continue on down the backs of the legs and through and out of the soles of your feet.

15. When you reach the soles of your feet again continue on down 3 feet (90 cm) below your body, beyond the edge of your energy field.

16. Let your hands, arms, body, and mind relax. Take some moments to savour the sensation and feeling.

17. Repeat this procedure at least twice more.

At the end of this whole sequence, which can be performed quickly or slowly depending on the time that you have available and the amount of attention that you want to give to it, you will have cleaned some of the negative energy which we all accumulate in normal life, out of your system. This is a wonderful thing to do. For the sake of a minuscule amount of effort in learning this very simple and straightforward sequence you can learn a skill which you can use for the rest of your life.

Do it every morning to start your day. Do it at night to relax, unwind and prepare to sleep. Do it any time you want. Doing this practice is like taking a shower – you end up clean, fresh and relaxed.

3

Oriental Energy – Anatomy and Physiology

THE AWARENESS OF CHI/ENERGY pervades everything in the Orient. It permeates every aspect of life. There are different kinds of chi for the weather, the environment, architecture, relationships between people, the economy, food, cars . . . There are as many kinds of chi as there are types of snow to an Eskimo. The nearest thing to chi in the West is describing how you 'feel' about something. Describing the chi of anything is like having a combination of a noun, verb and adjective; not having this is similar to not being able to describe colour. It is fundamental to the way that people in the East think, experience and behave, and astonishingly we have no real comparison.

In the human body, chi has an anatomy and physiology which follows a set of rules and laws as strict and fixed as Western anatomy and physiology. It is the foundation of acupuncture, it is what herbs act upon, it is what moves in Tai Chi Chuan exercises and it is what the practice of Chi Kung affects and develops.

The key to all of this is the anatomy and physiology of your energy system. The Oriental point of view is that the state of health is based in your meridian system, and that your chi can be guided and developed – internally by the mind and externally by movement. Chi Kung is one way for you to develop this for yourself.

It is essential for anyone wishing to understand Chi Kung to have a basic guide map of the anatomy (the structure) and physiology (how it works) of the energy system. Many of the concepts are unfamiliar to the Western way of thinking, and there are numerous words and names for the same thing, which differ according to the particular source or translation. However a broad sketch of the landscape will help us find our way around.

ENERGY ANATOMY

The primary features of Oriental energy anatomy are very different from anything we are familiar with in the West. However, they are the foundation of an understanding that has been the basis of health and well-being for a quarter of the world's population for the whole of recorded history. This cannot easily be dismissed as just 'weird'; it deserves our best attention.

The main features of this energy anatomy view of ourselves are: The Meridians; The Organs; The Points; The Three Chou; The Pulses; The Basic Substances; The Three Tan T'ien; The Three Treasures; and the Soul and Spirit.

THE MERIDIANS

The meridians are lines or channels in the body which conduct the chi/energy. In Oriental anatomy there is complete agreement from all authorities about the basic meridians/channels and their layout (although there are, of course, some very minor differences of opinion about details).

The meridians are a separate and discrete system in the body, independent of any of the other anatomical systems (the blood system, the nervous system, the lymphatic system . . .) although in many instances the meridian system runs parallel with, and is complementary to them. In some ways it can be considered as a 'control system' or a 'blueprint' which operates at a higher level, or octave, from the physical 'flesh and blood' level. In the body there is a hierarchy of control, as mentioned earlier, which can be described as operating in the following sequence:

Chi/Energy – Blood – Cells – Tissues – Organs – Functions – Relationships – The Whole

This sequence can be more fully described as: the chi leads the blood, the blood feeds the cells, the cells constitute the tissues, the tissues compose the organs, the organs carry out the functions and the functions together make up the Whole.

In Chi Kung, *the mind leads the chi*!

In total there are thirty-five meridians and together they constitute the complete anatomy of the chi meridian system. There are twelve major meridians/channels, eight extra meridians and fifteen

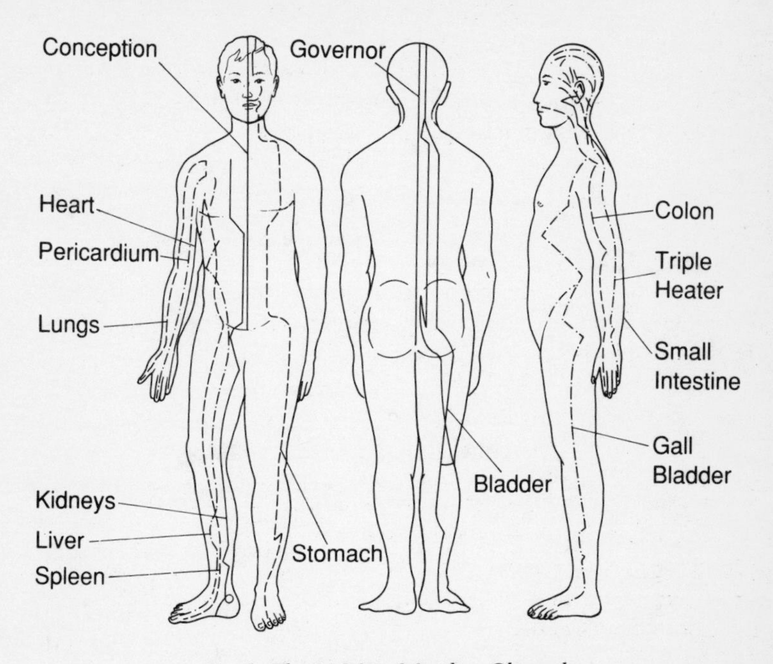

Fig. 5. The 14 Main Meridian Channels

collateral channels. The twelve major meridians and the two main extra meridians, which constitute the fourteen major channels, have along them a differing number of 'acupoints', which are the places where acupuncture, heat, massage or some form of stimulation or contact is applied to effect changes in the energy system. Together they connect every part of the body and make it an integrated whole.

The Twelve Major Meridians

The twelve major meridians are each related and connected to a specific organ, and in the West they are usually called by the name of the relevant organ. However, as we will see later in the Table of Correspondences (page 61), the meridian is not considered to relate solely to that particular organ but to many other aspects of the person as well, such as particular tissues, sense organs, emotions, faculties and so on.

The twelve major meridians have superficial and deep pathways, and connecting channels between them. On the superficial/surface level they form a continuous 'loop' or circuit with the end of one flowing into the beginning of the next, from the torso to the hands, to the head, to the feet, and back to the torso. It does this three times, for a total of twelve meridians. These are all bilateral, mirror images of each other on left and right side.

The Eight Extra Meridians

These are also sometimes known as the The Eight Extraordinary or The Eight Miraculous Meridians. These channels are considered to be the oceans of energy – reservoirs which can be drawn upon if there is a deficiency, or which can accommodate any excess. Together these extra meridians are the very basis of the initial stages of Chi Kung practice – they constitute its main 'framework' or skeleton. They are in four sets of pairs – The Governor and Conception Channels, The Thrusting and Girdle Channels, The Yin Wei and Yang Wei Channels and The Yin Qiao and Yang Qiao Channels.

The Governor and Conception Channels are the only other two channels, along with the twelve major organ channels, which have points along them. The Governor Channel runs up the centre of the back and over the head to end on the top lip and has twenty-eight points, and the Conception Channel runs up the centre of the front, ending on the bottom lip and has twenty-four points on it. The Governor and Conception Channels are fundamental to the first stages of Chi Kung practice in activating and circulating the Microcosmic Orbit or Small Heavenly Circuit.

The next pair of the eight extra meridians are the Thrusting Channel (or Chong Mo) and the Girdle Channel (or Dai Mo).

The Thrusting Channel runs directly up the centre of the body, from the perineum to the crown. It is about 3 inches (7.5 cm) wide and along it are all of the 'cauldrons'. These are approximately at the same horizontal level as the related points on the surface of the body on the Governor and Conception Channels. It is at these places that the chi/energy can be more easily felt and combined, changed or affected.

The Girdle Channel is usually understood as a belt, which runs around the waist, and is considered to tie the other meridians in. It is the only channel which runs horizontally around the body – all the others run vertically from top to bottom. In Chi Kung this 'belt channel' circulates not only at the waist, but envelopes the whole of the body from top to bottom, and outside of it to the edge of the bio-electromagnetic field, like a cocoon.

The final four extra meridians are known as the Yin Wei Mo and the Yang Wei Mo and The Yin Qiao Mo and Yang Qiao Mo. In Chi Kung practice they connect and link the arms and legs and everything else together.

The Other Channels

The other meridians are known as Lou Channels, or Junction Channels. Fourteen of them branch off from their respective main channels in the major meridians and the extra meridians, and act to connect each one with its specific coupled meridian; they connect Yang and Yin. This is like a brother-sister relationship between the various organs and extra meridians. There is one additional Lou Meridian which is the Great Envelope of the Spleen, which joins everything together, located under the armpit on the side of the chest.

Combined, these thirty-five meridian channels run throughout the body. They are the main pathways for the chi circulation; the chi flows out from them to all of the rest of the body – our cells, tissues, organs and functions. They cover the territory, connect everything together and make the body an integrated whole, with all of its parts connected to everything else.

THE ORGANS AND THE OFFICIALS

The twelve main meridians are each related to a particular organ, but classically these are considered not just to be the physical organs but also each one is seen as an 'official'. The brain and uterus are not considered as primary organs and they do not have meridians of their own. They are known as extraordinary organs, or peculiar organs, and are each affected by a number of different meridian systems which penetrate and permeate them.

Each official has responsibility for, and control over, a particular 'domain', just as in any society there are people responsible for certain functions in that society. Indeed, societies can be basically considered to be extensions out in the world of our internal functions. It appears that every society has the same basic functions which have to be taken care of – there is always somebody who is in command, there are people that are responsible for planning, there are people who dispose of the rubbish, others who look after transportation, and so on. When the whole operates in an integrated and comprehensive way then everything works the way it should. So it is with the officials and their meridians.

THE POINTS

The other aspect of the anatomy of the energy system that is critical to understanding how the energy operates is the 'points'. These are specific places on the surface of the body where the energy can be affected and changed, most familiar and well known through acupuncture. There are 670 commonly agreed points along the meridians, there are 'extra' points and there are an ever increasing number of 'new', or newly discovered, points. Each point has its own name; a categorization according to specific principles; a particular function; and in many cases a 'spirit of the point'. There are Junction points, Meeting points, Alarm points, Associated Effect points, Exit and Entry points, Collection points, Ashi points, 'Window of the Sky' points, Spirit points, and so on.

The Chi Kung Points

In Chi Kung there are certain major points which are used continuously. These are familiar to all Chi Kung practitioners: the navel, the crown, the perineum, the brow, the tongue, the palms, the soles of the feet, the kidney and the heart points. It is necessary to have a working understanding and knowledge of these major points in order to progress beyond repetitive learning. It is as essential to understand these nine basic points for any in-depth understanding and control of your chi, as it is to understand the muscle system to do massage, the skeleton to perform surgery or the musical scales to sing or play the saxophone. These could be called *The Chi Kung Points* (see Figure 6).

THE THREE CHOU

Another important and unique structure of Oriental anatomy is the way in which the torso is divided into three separate sections. These are known as The Three Chou. The lower chou is the area below the navel. The middle chou is from the navel to the diaphragm at the base of the rib cage. The upper chou is the area from the diaphragm to

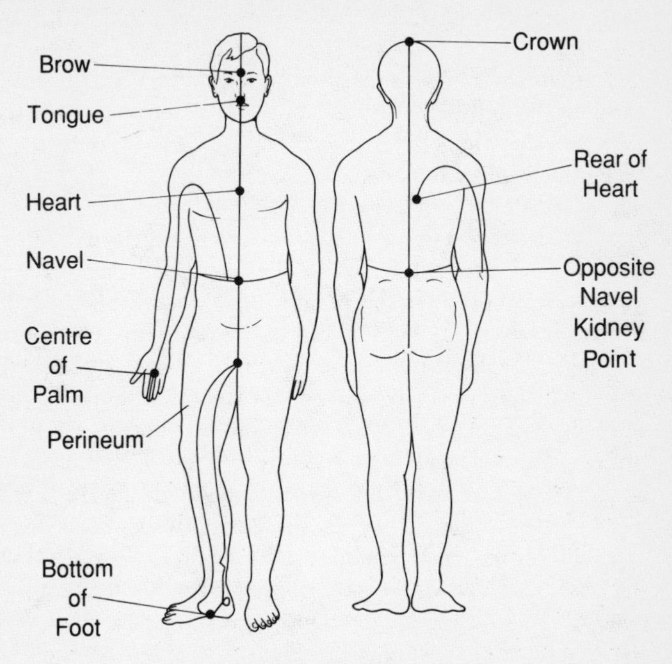

Fig. 6. The Major Chi Kung Points

the neck. Each of these areas operates at a separate and independent temperature, and each governs the particular internal organs and functions in that area, so the right balance and integration between them is essential.

THE PULSES

So how is this all understood? How does somebody know what state and condition a person's meridians are in, or what is happening to the organs/officials? What is the quality and character of someone's chi/energy? This brings us to one of the most astonishing and unique characteristics of the meridian system and Oriental medicine – the pulses.

The pulses are the basic way in which the chi in the twelve major meridians, and therefore the energy of a person, is read and monitored. Each of the twelve organs/officials has a separate and distinct pulse, which can be felt and 'read' by the fingertips of a trained and experienced practitioner. The pulses are located on the radial artery of the wrist (but may also be felt at the ankle and neck). There are three positions on each wrist, one at the normal position for feeling the heart-rate pulse, opposite the styloid process, (position 2 in Figure 7), then another one finger-tip in front of this, and the third position one finger-tip behind. In each position there are two levels – one superficial, the other deep, so therefore there are six positions on each wrist, for a total of twelve on both wrists together. The positions, levels and related organs/officials are shown in Figure 8.

Each of these separate pulses is classically described as having twenty-eight different qualities that can be felt; these are described in terms such as floating or sinking, hard or soft, fast or slow, large or small, full or empty, and so on. And then there are combinations of qualities – so a particular pulse/organ may be sinking, hard and slow, or floating, soft and empty, for example. In this way it is possible to know the nature of the chi in a particular organ, and therefore its state and condition.

This technique can reveal information about the person that the most sophisticated scientific technology currently available cannot. It is so pervasive and accepted in the East that often people will refer to going to see a doctor as '. . . going to get my pulses read'. It is one of the most revealing and comprehensive techniques known, and is limited only by the skill and experience of the practitioner. The legend is that it requires ten years of continual practice to learn how to read the pulses correctly, comparable, perhaps, to the experience needed to play the concert piano or violin.

THE BASIC SUBSTANCES – CHI, BLOOD AND FLUIDS

Chi, blood and fluids are fundamental substances in the human body. They are derived from the essence of breathing, eating and drinking – the usual ways in which we take energy from the outside (external chi) into ourselves – and sustain normal vital functions. They nourish and lubricate the organs and tissues. The quality of the chi determines the quality of the blood, and the quality of the blood determines the quality of the chi; stagnation in one will cause stagnation in the other. Both are food for the cells of which we are made, so having good quality in them is essential for health and vitality.

The essence of food and drink is also transformed into body fluids. There are two types of fluids, thin and thick. The thin type warms and nourishes the muscles and moistens the skin. The thick type lubricates the joints and moistens the orifices. Body fluids are also the basic constituent of the sweat, urine, saliva and, of course, the

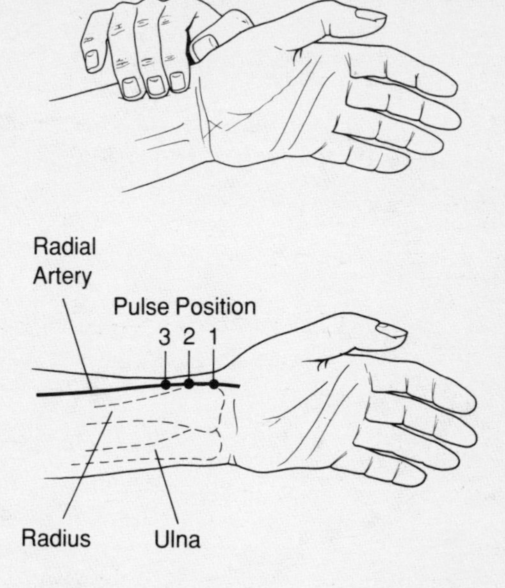

Fig. 7. Taking 'The Pulses' at the Wrist

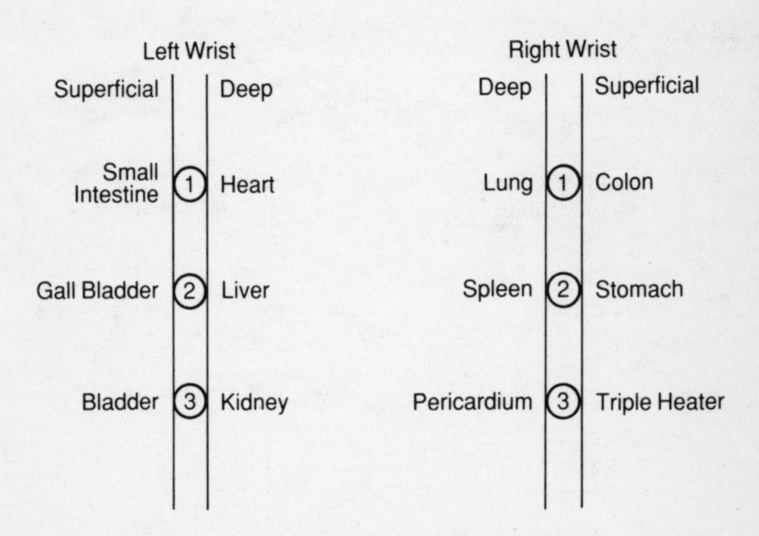

Fig. 8. Pulse Positions and their Correspondences

blood. So body fluids are basic to good functioning and provide the foundational substance for everything else.

THE THREE TAN T'IEN

The Three Tan T'ien are also known as the Three Fields of Cultivation. This refers to three areas of the body – on the lower abdomen where one's power is stored, on the middle abdomen where one's emotions and chi reside, and in the centre of the head where mental and spiritual dimensions are developed. These are the areas where The Three Treasures are cultivated.

THE THREE TREASURES

Underlying all of these structures and functions, at a more primary level, is a way in which the Orientals understand the totality of the human being. They categorize us as having three basic components, or levels, known as The Three Treasures, because a depletion or

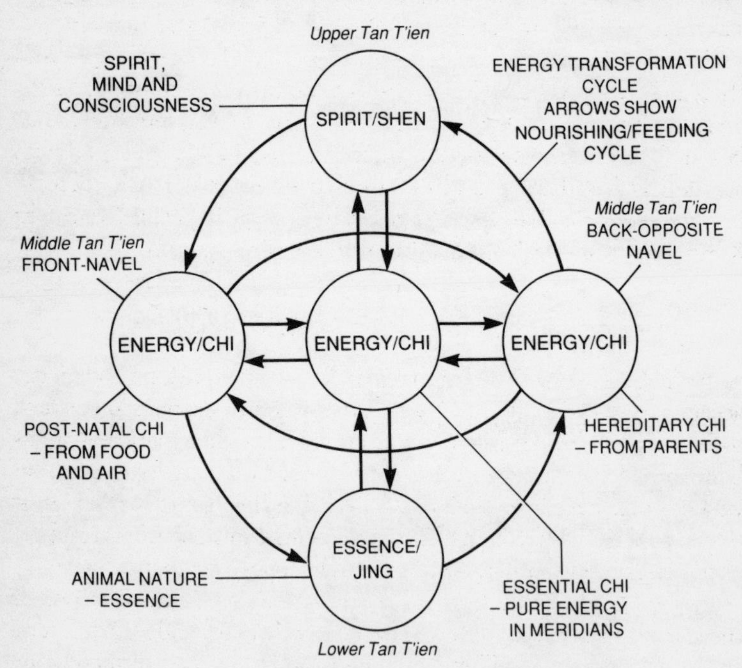

Fig. 9. The Three Treasures and their Transformations
Essence – Energy – Spirit Jing – Chi – Shen

deficiency in any of these will undermine our whole being. These are called Jing, Chi and Shen.

Jing is the inherited genetic energy from our parents and ancestors and also our sexual energy, which it is vital to preserve. There are many practices to conserve and preserve this Jing in Chinese sexual manuals. Males have Yang Jing and females have Yin Jing, each of which needs aspects of the other to stay balanced and healthy – hence one reason for the popularity of sex throughout history.

Chi, as described previously, is the 'stuff' that we run on. It has many different forms – ta chi, ku chi, yuan chi, jing chi, wei chi and so on. It can be depleted by overwork, malnourishment, wrong habits and too much sex. It is developed, in part, from Jing Chi, which provides the foundation for it.

Shen is a general term for spirit. The spirit is fed and nourished by the chi. The spirit body is of a higher level or frequency than the chi and is dependent upon it. It is said to reside in the heart, and a person's Shen can easily be seen in their eyes. Someone with good Shen has eyes that sparkle and are alive, while a person with poor Shen has dull eyes which seem to be covered over and hidden.

So Jing, Chi and Shen are hierarchically based on each other, and there are things we can do to preserve, nourish and cultivate them, and also things which will empty, deplete and undermine them. For a Chi Kung practitioner their actions, habits and practices are largely based upon and determined by whatever will increase or decrease these Three Treasures. They are as important to a Chi Kung practitioner as credit rating is to a businessperson!

SOUL AND SPIRIT

Spirit is a general term used in the West for which there is no commonly accepted simple definition. However the spirit is the glue that has held together not only all spiritual traditions, but also whole nations – it has built cathedrals, launched wars, and provided the very foundation on which people have lived their entire lives. It is the instinctive and intuitive experience of the eternal fragment of the universe which each of us possesses inside. It may be the most precious thing that we have.

In the Oriental tradition there are various subtle distinctions of the spirit, subdivisions of it, which reside within us, and also different categories of the soul. There are understood to be five spirits – Hun, Shen, Yi, Po, Zhi – and each one is related to the organs/officials of the liver, heart, spleen, lungs and kidneys respectively. By purifying, nourishing and refining these organs through specific formulas and procedures, one develops the Virtues. There are also various souls, which are similarly cultivated.

There is a corresponding energetic dimension of this, which could be described as having one's energy operating at a higher and cleaner frequency. That is one of the primary things that the Taoist monks are doing in the monasteries: actual practices and procedures that purify and raise the quality and frequency of their energy, in order to develop their soul and spirit. However, the anatomy and physiology of the soul and the spirit are subjects worthy of greater attention than can be devoted here. In the Oriental tradition there is indeed a thorough understanding of this, and it forms the foundation for the spiritual aspect and tradition of Chi Kung practice.

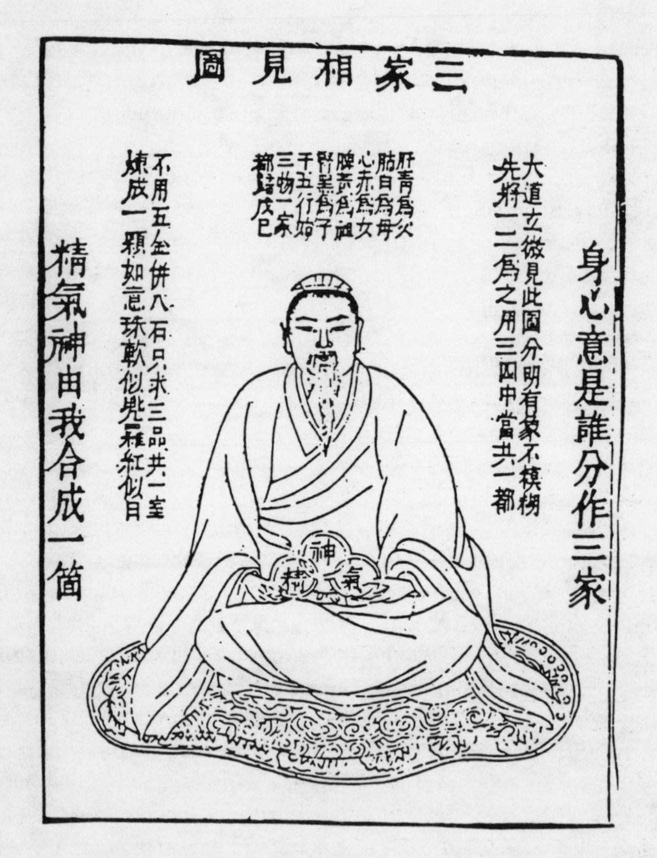

Fig. 10. Traditional Woodcut Depicting the Union of the Three Treasures

YOUR ENERGY ANATOMY AND CHI KUNG

Although this may all seem unfamiliar and strange, these anatomical features – the meridians, the organs, the points, the three chou, the pulses, the basic substances, the three tan t'ien, the three treasures and the spirit and soul – are the basic structure of our chi/energy system, and therefore also the practice of Chi Kung. Now let's look at how it all works.

ENERGY PHYSIOLOGY

The physiology of the energy system – how it works – is the reflection of its laws and principles. These are based on the laws of nature and Chi Kung operates according to these laws. The major features of this are: The Tao; Yin and Yang; The Five Elements; The Table of Correspondence; Family Relations; Natural Cycles and Biorhythms; and The Factors of Disease. Understanding and recognizing these gives us a deep sense of our inherent functioning and how we are intrinsically connected to the whole of nature, and indicates what we may do to align ourselves with it.

THE TAO

Our physiology operates according to the principles of the Tao, which have been described earlier. This is the origin and the nature of all things. Chi Kung could be described as 'The Tao in Action'.

YIN AND YANG AND THE EIGHT PRINCIPLES

The symbol of the Tao is seen in the well-known image of the two interlocking fishes. One is white and the other is black and they represent the basic polarity of opposites, known as the Yin and the Yang. This polarity includes all things.

To our common perception everything is complemented by its opposite – up/down, black/white, day/night, positive/negative, male/female, movement/stillness, growth/decay . . . These principles operate according to very specific natural laws. The most fundamental of these are called the laws of Yin/Yang. There are many variations of Yin/Yang; indeed, ancient philosophers and court advisors maintained their livelihood and position by extending and describing the subtleties of interaction and interchange of Yin/Yang.

Fig. 11. The Tao and Yin/Yang

Yin and Yang polarity form the basis in Oriental physiology of what is known as The Eight Principles. This is a way of understanding and describing the state and condition of the chi according to eight parameters. There are four pairs of opposites – Yin/Yang, Interior/Exterior, Deficiency/Excess, and Cold/Hot. For instance, a person may have an internal energy condition which could be described as Yin, interior, deficient and cold or Yang, exterior, excessive and hot. In a practical sense this allows for a way of thinking about a specific condition or situation and therefore being able to decide on a course of action to take that would resolve the differences and bring things back into balance.

Five major principles of Yin/Yang have been recognized, which describe their interaction: everything has a Yin and Yang aspect; every Yin and Yang can be further divided; Yin and Yang create each other; Yin and Yang control each other; Yin and Yang can each transform into the other.

THE FIVE ELEMENTS – WOOD, FIRE, EARTH, METAL, WATER

After the division into Yin and Yang the Taoists divide all things into The Five Elements. This is a way of understanding and describing the nature of things in basic categories according to their inherent qualities. There are many ways in which the Five Elements can interact together, and these differences form the basis for whole schools of thought in Taoism.

It is perhaps easiest to understand the Five Elements in relationship to the seasons of the year. The succession of the seasons is the basic condition under which all life has evolved. This is so fundamental that we tend not even to notice it as being our primary pre-condition; just as if we asked fish what it was like to swim in water, they might answer, incomprehensibly, 'what's water?' The seasons are based on the rotation of the earth around the sun. They always follow the same sequence, always have and always will. They never miss a season, or jump one or go in the opposite direction. They are stable and predictable and provide the basic metronome of life. Although in the West we consider there to be four seasons, the Orientals have five. The familiar Western sequence is Spring, Summer, Autumn and Winter; however, the Orientals consider the period of Late-Summer (sometimes called Indian Summer) to be a separate and distinct season of its own, the point of balance and harmony of the year – the Centre Place.

Each of these seasons has a particular quality to it, which reflects its character and nature. Each of these qualities is described in terms of an Element or Phase. These Five Elements translate as Wood, Fire, Earth, Metal and Water. Wood is the power or force which motivates things to grow in the Spring; Fire is the heat and

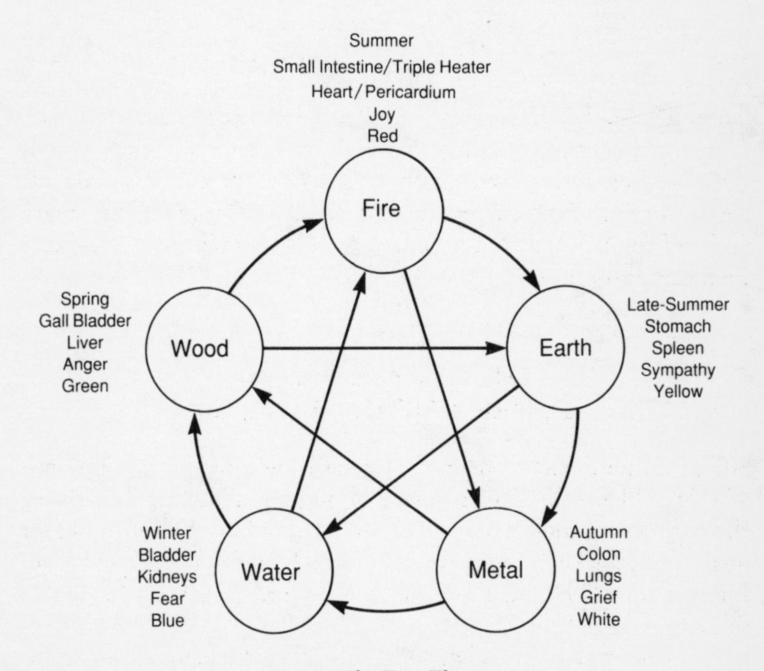

Fig. 12. The Five Elements

activity which reaches a peak in Summer; Earth is the ground which provides a foundation for everything, reaching the centre point of Late Summer; Metal is the minerals which return to the ground in Autumn; Water is the snow and ice of Winter.

The Five Elements and seasons also have corresponding organs and emotions related to each one. For Spring/Wood the organs are the Liver and the Gall Bladder and the emotion is Anger/Power; for Summer/Fire they are the Heart and Small Intestines, the Pericardium and Triple Heater and the emotion is Joy/Love; for Late Summer/Earth it is the Spleen-Pancreas and the Stomach and the emotion is Sympathy/Compassion; for Autumn/Metal it is the Lungs and the Colon and the emotion is Grief/Cleansing; for Winter/Water it is the Kidneys and the Bladder and the emotion is Fear/Awe.

In addition to all of this there are many more relationships of the Five Elements which are illustrated in the Table of Correspondences (see figure 13). These relationships are expanded into many other aspects of life, and provide the basic foundation for this comprehensive and integrated way of looking at, and experiencing, the world.

TABLE OF CORRESPONDENCES

The Table of Correspondences is the classical Oriental way of understanding our holistic nature and the relationship between all of our different parts. This way of seeing things ties all of the different aspects of ourselves into one integrated and interrelated whole, for example; the physical level of organs, senses, tissues, functions; the emotional level of our basic feelings; the mental level of our abilities of planning, decision making, willpower, differentiation, sorting, control and so on; and the various dimensions and levels of our spirit.

The Table of Correspondences also extends into the relationships of colours, sounds, odours, times of day, flavours, and so on. It is an understanding of the relationships of all our parts, and therefore is one of the original holistic views of the world. It is Internal Ecology. It is worthy of our best attention and consideration. It provides a foundation for an integrated view and comprehension of who and what we are, and how we operate and function, which has withstood the most rigorous test and scrutiny of all – the test of time.

THE TABLE OF CORRESPONDENCES & THE FIVE ELEMENTS

ELEMENT	WOOD	FIRE	EARTH	METAL	WATER
SEASON	Spring	Summer	Late Summer	Autumn	Winter
YANG ORGAN	Gall Bladder	Small Intestine Triple Heater	Stomach	Colon	Bladder
YIN ORGAN	Liver	Heart Pericardium	Spleen	Lungs	Kidneys
EMOTION	Anger	Joy	Sympathy	Grief	Fear
COLOUR	Green	Red	Yellow	White	Blue
SOUND	Shouting	Laughing	Singing	Weeping	Groaning
TASTE	Sour	Bitter	Sweet	Pungent	Salty
SMELL	Rancid	Scorched	Fragrant	Rotten	Putrid
OPENING	Eyes	Tongue	Mouth	Nose	Ears
TISSUE	Tendons	Blood Vessels	Flesh	Skin and Hair	Bones
CLIMATE	Wind	Heat	Damp	Dry	Cold
PROCESS	Birth	Growth	Transformation	Harvest	Storage
DIRECTION	East	South	Centre	West	North

LAWS AND PRINCIPLES – FAMILY RELATIONSHIPS

A number of the basic laws and principles of the chi meridian system reflect the relationships of our most fundamental unit – the family.

Mother/Child

The Law of Mother/Child is one of those principles of Taoist philosophy which are based on the most obvious relationships and patterns in the ordinary everyday world, but which are often unrecognized and unappreciated. The Mother/Child Law is part of the Five Elements system (see figure 12). It is also known as the Shen Cycle, or the Nurturing Cycle, which in its simplest form states that each organ/official is the mother of the organ/official following it, and the child of the one preceding it. According to this cycle each official is 'fed' or nurtured by the one that feeds into it, just as a mother is responsible for nourishing her own child. Therefore, if the mother is not functioning properly in a healthy way – either too weak or too strong – then the child will be correspondingly affected, and vice versa.

There are also permutations of Grandmother/Grandchild which operate in the same way as normal life. One variation of this Family Relations which is missing in the Taoist system, and which is critical to many people's lives, is the Law of Mother-in-Law/Son-in-Law!

Husband/Wife

The relationship of husband-wife/man-woman is the foundation from which we all come. To the Taoist viewpoint this is a reflection of the relationship between Yin and Yang, which has to have a particular dynamic and balance in order for movement to take place. If Yin and Yang are perfectly balanced there would be no activity, just stagnation. To be in the correct relationship the Yang has to be slightly stronger than the Yin. If the Yin is stronger than the Yang the dynamic is not right and it is a very serious condition which, if not corrected, will cause problems in a person's energy system.

Brothers/Sisters

All organs are paired in couples, according to their Five Element relationship. These are Liver and Gall Bladder in Wood, Heart and Small Intestine, Pericardium and Triple Heater in Fire, Spleen and

Stomach in Earth, Lungs and Colon in Metal, and Kidneys and Bladder in Water. These couples have a sister/brother, Yin/Yang, relationship.

NATURAL CYCLES AND BIORHYTHMS – THE EARTH, MOON AND SUN

Many aspects of the body are based on natural cycles – the rhythms and regularities of nature. Our bodies evolved over millions of years within the context of the earth, moon and sun cycles. We experience these from our own perspective as the alternations of day and night, the twenty-eight day moon cycle and the cycle of the seasons. As these rhythms come and go we are profoundly affected by them, but this is unconscious for most people. By knowing these natural cycles we can attune ourselves to the inherent rhythms of our own energy as it moves inside us, and thereby attune to nature.

The Earth and Day/Night

There are twenty-four hours in each day and there are twelve major organs in the body. The chi flows in the meridians and organs continuously but reaches a peak in each organ for two hours in each day; therefore in one day it moves like a tidal wave through all of the organs. This is the same for everyone and relates to the position of the sun. At these specific times of the day it is possible to affect the relevant organ more.

The sequence is:

Heart	11am – 1pm	Gall Bladder	11pm – 1am
Small Intestine	1pm – 3pm	Liver	1am – 3am
Bladder	3pm – 5pm	Lungs	3am – 5am
Kidneys	5pm – 7pm	Colon	5am – 7am
Pericardium	7pm – 9pm	Stomach	7am – 9am
Triple Heater	9pm – 11pm	Spleen	9am – 11am

In fact, the ancient Chinese clock consisted of just twelve units in a day, with each unit consisting of two of our contemporary hours:

Wu	–	11am – 1pm	Zi	–	11pm – 1am
Wei	–	1pm – 3pm	Chou	–	1am – 3am
Shen	–	3pm – 5pm	Yin	–	3am – 5am
You	–	5pm – 7pm	Mao	–	5am – 7am
Xu	–	7pm – 9pm	Chen	–	7am – 9am
Hai	–	9pm – 11pm	Si	–	9am – 11am

This reflects the biological fact of energy movement in our bodies and organs. The significance and importance of this is obviously enormous, as it affects all of our daily functions, abilities and moods, and yet generally in the West we have no awareness or understanding of it at all!

The Moon and The Month

Every twenty-eight days the chi completes one cycle up the back and down the front of the body, in the Governor and Conception channels. At the full moon the chi is at its peak, the crown of the head, at the empty moon it is at the perineum. This moon circulation controls the tides and women's menstrual cycle.

The Sun and The Seasons

In each season the chi also reaches a peak in a pair of organs – Gall Bladder and Liver in the Spring, Small Intestine and Heart (and Pericardium and Triple Heater) in the Summer, Stomach and Spleen in the Late Summer, Colon and Lungs in the Autumn, and Bladder and Kidneys in the Winter. In this way the seasons have a profound effect on us. Any Western doctor will tell you how certain organs have symptoms at particular times of the year – this circulation of energy is the reason why.

FACTORS OF DISEASE

So where does imbalance and disease come from? How is it people become ill? Why does the chi become dysfunctional? There are two basic causes of disease – external and internal.

External factors can include: adverse environmental conditions of heat, cold, wind, dryness and humidity; wrong diet; spoiled food; worms and microbes; poisoning and pollution; trauma and accidents. Internal conditions can arise from excess or deficient emotions of anger, joy, sympathy, grief or fear – which in turn can be generated from the emotional environment you are in. They can be caused by inappropriate mental attitudes and beliefs. There are also maladies of the spirit which can cause serious problems. These factors can cause

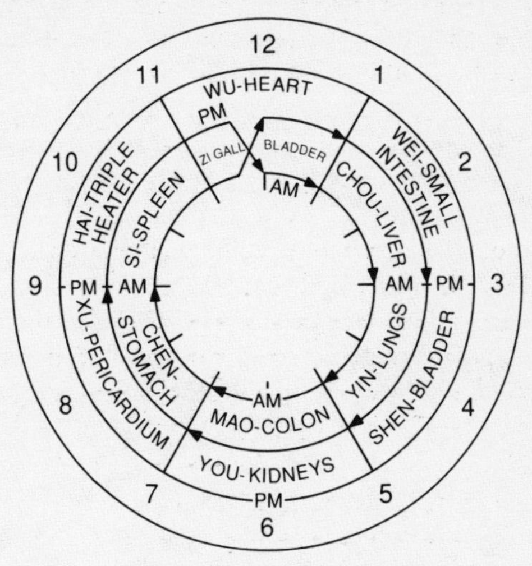

Fig. 14. The Biological Energy Clock
The Watch Face of the Future?

one's chi to become excessive, deficient, stuck, blocked, congested or stagnant, and thereby cause all manner of problems. A wide range of factors can cause one's chi to become out of order and therefore set the ground for illness and dysfunction. Knowing and understanding these, and avoiding factors that cause problems, can be a major aspect of preserving your chi.

YOUR ENERGY ANATOMY AND PHYSIOLOGY AND CHI KUNG

The physiology is how your energy works. The laws and principles of the Tao, Yin and Yang, the Five Elements, the Table of Correspondence, Family Relations, Natural Cycles and the Factors of Disease are ways in which your energy operates. Knowing, respecting and aligning yourself with these will help you to preserve your chi.

Understanding the anatomy and physiology of the chi/energy

system will help you to maintain and develop your health and your state of being. Chi Kung allows you to do this for yourself.

EXERCISE THREE

Focusing at Your Body Energy Centre

Concentrate your chi into your Centre Place, and store it there.

Purpose
An internal Nei Dan practice to increase the general volume of your energy, to 'ground' you, to keep you 'centred' by bringing energy to your actual physical centre and to give you a way to 'check-in' with yourself.

The sequence
1. Sit on the edge of a chair, knees parallel, shoulder-width apart and bent at right angles, feet flat on the floor. This exercise can also be done lying down. Place your right hand facing down, over your left hand facing upwards, and let your clasped hands rest gently in your lap. Clear your mind of extraneous thoughts and visualize a blue cloudless sky.

2. You are going to create a 'Pa Kua' – a pattern of three concentric, eight-sided shapes/octagons, one inside the other – around your navel. To learn how to create this pattern, and train your mind, you will begin by first using a finger to draw imaginary lines on your abdomen around your navel. Then, after practice, you can create it by just using your mind alone.

3. Looking down at your navel imagine it is a clock-face, with the navel as the centre – twelve o'clock at the top, three o'clock to the left-hand side, six o'clock at the bottom and nine o'clock on the right-hand side.

4. Do this exercise with half-closed eyes – half outward-focused looking at and watching what you are doing, half inward-focused, feeling the sensation that you are experiencing. Later, when you are familiar with the procedure, do it with your eyes fully closed, so that you can concentrate on the sensation and experience. In this way you will educate and train your mind about the experience and feeling, and learn how to control and direct your energy with your mind alone.

5. Place a finger on your abdomen 3 inches (7.5 cm) above your navel at twelve o'clock. All of the lines on this octagon, 3 inches from your

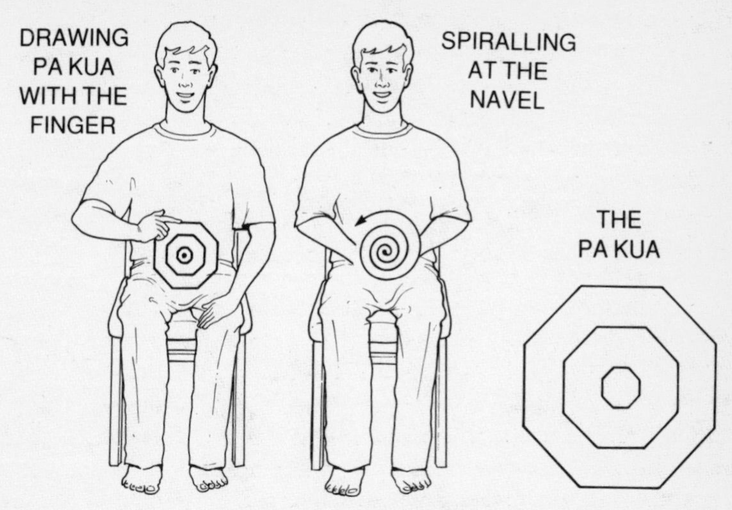

Fig. 15. Focusing at the Centre

navel, are about 2½ inches (6 cm) long. To get to the starting position of this top line, come back to your right about 1¼ inches (3 cm).

(a) With the tip of your finger go from right to left and draw a horizontal line across the top.
(b) Moving in a clockwise direction draw another line diagonally downwards.
(c) Next, draw a line vertically down from top to bottom on the left side, at the three o'clock position.
(d) Then, angle diagonally inwards and down.
(e) Next, draw a line horizontally across the bottom from left to right at the six o'clock position.
(f) Then, angle diagonally up towards the right.
(g) Draw vertically up, from bottom to top, at the nine o'clock position.
(h) Finally, angle diagonally inwards and upwards, to join the right side starting position of the original horizontal line across the top.

You have now completed the first and outer-most octagon of the Pa Kua.

6. Repeat the above sequence, only this time just 2 inches (5 cm) from the navel. Each line is approximately 1½ inches (4 cm) long.

7. Repeat the above sequence, but this time only 1 inch (2.5 cm) from the navel. Each line is approximately ¾ inch (2 cm) long.

8. Again draw three concentric octagons of 3, 2 and 1 inches (7.5 cm,

5 cm and 2.5 cm) from the centre of your navel *but this time just with your mind.* Close your eyes and concentrate. Repeat this over and over until you can feel and sense it clearly. In this way you will begin to educate and train your mind alone to draw the Pa Kua, and thereby train your mind to direct and control your chi/energy.

9. Repeat this until you can do it at will. If you lose the sense of it then go back to doing it with your finger. For a more direct experience try doing it directly on your skin, not through clothing. Repeat it until you 'get it'. By doing this procedure you form a 'net' or web around your navel, which can collect energy there. (Pa Kuas are wonderful energy collection patterns. You can also use Pa Kuas at any other points to concentrate your energy there.)

10. Now, you will learn to activate and 'open' your energy – in order to turn it 'ON'. Using the tip of a finger start in the centre of your navel and begin to spiral outwards, keeping your finger flat on your clothes or skin, in ever-increasing and expanding spirals. Men go out in an anticlockwise direction, from twelve o'clock to nine to six to three and back to twelve. Women go in a clockwise direction from twelve o'clock to three to six to nine and back to twelve again. Move from the centre all the way out to the edge of the base of the ribs at twelve o'clock, and the top of the pubic bone at six o'clock. Do nine spirals out and then reverse the direction for six spirals in. Whilst doing this maintain the visual image of the Pa Kua energy net.

Spiralling in this direction opens the energy centre and activates it. Finally to seal it, put the centre of one palm over your navel, with the centre of the other palm on top of it. Left hand first for men. Right hand first for women. Concentrate your mind into the navel point, and imagine that you are breathing into it. It is also *most* important to close the energy centre down after you have finished. Therefore, after you have opened this energy centre up, you *must* reverse the direction in order to bring your energy back safely to your centre, otherwise it will be opened up and maybe uncontrolled, and can cause detrimental effects.

11. This whole procedure brings the energy into the navel, which is the primary centre and storehouse/holding place for your energy. This is where the pre-natal chi first entered into you, as an embryo in the womb. It is Home-Base. If you simply concentrate your energy there it will be safe and stable.

To take this procedure further, and concentrate your energy even more strongly, condense your Pa Kua into a 1½ inch (4 cm) diameter.

To develop even more concentration and power spiral out thirty-six times and in twenty-four times.

To gather more energy into you, use your mind to draw external chi – from the sunlight, grass, trees and flowers, moon, stars, heavens, cosmos – into yourself.

Use this every day. Use it whenever you are feeling 'unbalanced' or 'ungrounded' to get you back into your centre.

Once you have mastered the ability to do this procedure with just your mind you can use it to check-in to yourself. If it is difficult to do because your energy feels too wild and out of control, or because it is too sluggish and won't move easily, take this as feedback to yourself about how your general energy is doing. By concentrating and establishing control over the Pa Kua you can thereby establish control of your whole energy.

You can also use this procedure to build up your energy and increase its volume.

Use it whenever you need to. Use it before going to sleep. Put it on automatic and have it happen all the time, by itself.

Forming and activating the Pa Kua around your navel is one of the most important and primary techniques that you can use to control, increase and re-charge your own energy. Try it and see for yourself.

4

The Different Kinds of Chi Kung and Their Applications

A COMPLETE TOOLBOX

CHI KUNG IS a miraculous, mysterious thing that can be used for all kinds of reasons. It is like a toolbox in which there are many different tools, all with different purposes. Some of them are simple and straightforward, their use is obvious and anybody can use them easily; others are so complicated that you need very specialized instruction by somebody who is trained and experienced. Each of these tools has a very particular application. It is as important to understand the right technique or method as it is to pick the right tool; you would not try to undo a screw with a hammer nor would you be advised to enter a martial arts competition having only trained in a Chi Kung method for longevity.

Clearly understanding your purpose and reason for practice is of primary importance, and the correct method and application has to be chosen and followed very specifically. It all depends on what it is that you want to achieve. The more simple and broadly based something is, then the more people can do it; the more refined and specialized then generally the fewer people who are interested in it or who can gain access to it. Millions of people can do simple standing postures which require minimal instruction, and thereby gain general benefits to their health and strength by increasing their volume of energy, while only the select few are initiated into the higher levels of inner alchemy in the monastic tradition for spiritual cultivation.

The applications of Chi Kung are very broad. Information available today ranges from books which you can buy in almost any bookshop; video tapes showing each move of a particular form that you can follow in your own home; weekly, weekend or extended courses, workshops or training programmes . . . There are programmes of every shape and size offered by teachers of every level of experience and accomplishment (see the Resource Directory at the back of this book). The indications are that these opportunities will continue to increase at an ever-accelerating rate.

A COMPENDIUM OF APPLICATIONS

The following is a compendium of the applications of Chi Kung. It is not intended to reflect any one particular bias that I may have, nor is it intended to exclude anything that I have become aware of during the research on this project. Some things may seem so obvious that you may question why they are being stated; other things so fantastic that you wonder if I have any critical judgement at all. All of that is beside the point of simply reporting what I have come to be aware of and understand. The following list is one possible categorization (my own) of the various and different applications of Chi Kung. This is presented in the interests of greater clarity and in

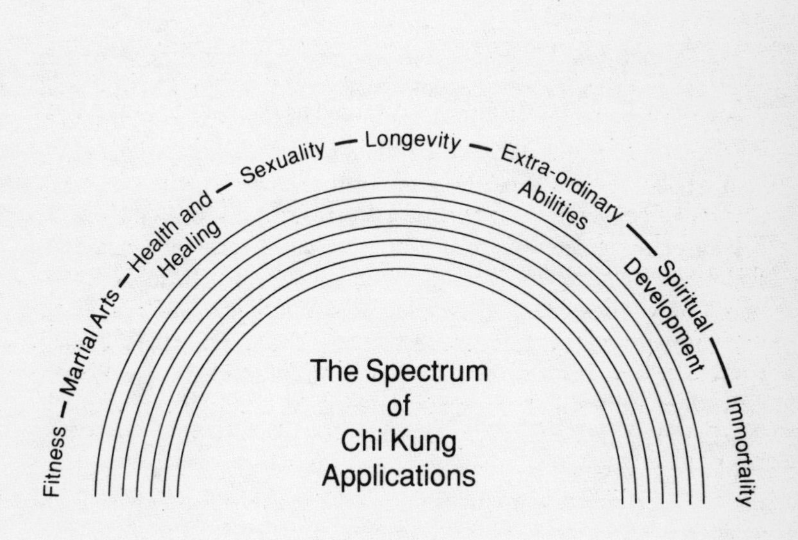

Fig. 16. The Spectrum of Chi Kung Applications

order to let you know what is generally available. The broad span of applications are for:

- Fitness
- Martial Arts
- Health and Healing
- Sex
- Longevity
- Extra-ordinary Human Abilities
- Spiritual Development
- Immortality

Within this framework and classification the following is a description and explanation of these various applications.

CHI KUNG FOR FITNESS

There are many applications of Chi Kung for fitness. Saying that you are using chi/energy for fitness in China is like saying you use muscles for exercise in the West – it is nonsensical to try to separate the two. The most visible and remarkable examples, of course, are The Peking Acrobats, those ambassadors of astonishment and wonder who seem to do things that no other group from any other country does. Anybody who has seen this troupe of performers is left in a state of slack-jawed wonder; it is just not possible for the human body to do what they do, yet there they are doing it. What is their secret? Take a wild guess!

Anybody who watched the finals of the 1988 Olympic Women's Volleyball between the USA and China, saw Chi Kung in action. For all of their determination, gung-ho gut-level high-five hand-slapping 110 per cent commitment and individualistic heroism, the Americans seemed to be playing a different game. None of the Chinese women individually stood out, but the ball seemed to move by itself from one player to another and the points just kept climbing – right up to the gold medal. How did they do it? Well, it certainly wasn't by eating Mars Bars!

Maybe one day TV will be able to show the chi-field in sports events, computer colour-enhanced of course; perhaps they will even be able to delete the figures of the individual players so that you can just watch the dance of multi-coloured energy. One thing that we know for sure is that when the National Football League in America and the Football Association in England and all of the other professional Sports

Associations in the world finally discover Chi Kung, there's going to be no lack of jobs for Chi Kung Masters-cum-coaches.

Long established in the Orient at all levels of society – from morning 'stretches' to full workouts – this form of exercise is very swiftly entering into the mainstream here. In the YMCA in San Francisco, right there among the nautilus equipment and stairmasters, on the sheet which told about alternative exercise, it listed four options, three of them now very familiar and ordinary, but the fourth was new – Yoga, Karate, Tai Chi and now . . . Chi Kung. The *San Francisco Chronicle*, a major international newspaper, recently ran a full article on Chi Kung, *in the sports section*. On the front cover was a picture of a running back from the San Francisco 49'ers Football Team in ecstatic air-pumping gladiator triumph after scoring a touch-down with all of his enormous power bursting out of his body; the newspaper copy-writer forgot to mention that this is a classic Chi Kung pose. Inside, in the story about Chi Kung, there were pictures of people serenely standing in postures among natural beauty and absorbing the energy of the grass, trees and nature into their bodies.

There are classic sets for health and fitness – self-massage, the Ba Duan Jin (The Eight Pieces of Brocade), the Wu Qin Xi (Five Animal Frolics), Wild Goose Chi Kung, Flying Crane Chi Kung, Swimming Dragon Chi Kung . . . specific exercise sequences each with its own purpose and benefits. Knowing these sets requires skills, discipline and training which are held in high esteem in the Orient.

It is absolutely certain that here in the West within the next few years endless gorgeous actresses and models will come out with their own fluorescent-lycra fashioned Chi Kung videos, afternoon TV shows will feature hour-long shots of delicate Oriental ladies sitting in complete stillness and Chi Kung will replace aerobics as the next health-club craze. Evolution works in strange ways!

CHI KUNG AND THE MARTIAL ARTS

The martial arts are peculiarly Oriental. Although all other cultures have fighting forms, in China this has been elevated to a national obsession. There seems to be little, if any, history of competitive sports in China, at least as far as is commonly known to the West. The development of excellence in 'physical culture' is concentrated into fighting, to the extent that it is considered an 'Art'.

Following the arrival of the Buddhist teacher Da Mo from India, circa AD 500, at the Shaolin Temple, the monks began to cultivate physical strength through the Muscle and Tendon Changing training and Bone Marrow Cleansing (which uses methods to clean accumulated fat from the centre of the bones and thereby produces plentiful clean, fresh blood cells, which is one of the 'secrets' of longevity). The Shaolin Temple became famous for its martial arts styles, using many secret techniques.

Another application of Martial Arts Chi Kung became known as 'Hard Chi Kung'. Practitioners demonstrate remarkable feats of strength and ability, which are sometimes performed in China like street side-shows for tips and donations from passers-by. By developing the ability to direct their energy to any one single point, practitioners are able to do such things as break thick slabs of rock with their head, bend long spears by pushing against the sharpened points with their neck, lie on beds of sharpened knives, balance upside down on one finger for long periods . . . and other such useful activities! Martial Arts Chi Kung also developed the strong body, or 'Iron Shirt Training' to be able to take hard blows without damaging essential internal organs. Iron Shirt training uses the internal energy to strengthen the fascia which surrounds all of the muscles and organs, thereby developing an impenetrable defence. It is said that such training can allow somebody to take a full-force blow in the face without even bruising.

A further application is in Tai Chi Chuan, the elegant and graceful flowing 'shadow boxing' that is one of the most familiar examples of Oriental Arts in the West. There are two distinct applications of Tai Chi Chuan; one is indeed for health and fitness, usually practised by older people, and commonly known as 'Tai Chi Chi Kung'. The other form is very definitely used for combat and fighting. Indeed, high-level Masters are said to fight without making physical contact or sometimes without even moving, just standing opposite each other waiting for a break or opening in the other's energy field. The rivalry among competing martial arts schools, styles and traditions is severe and intense. In martial arts circles there are innumerable stories of 'showdowns', when so-and-so fought so-and-so, re-told with the enthusiasm and awe of football fans talking about tough games.

Of the people the author contacted in researching information for this book, at least one-third of the non-Asians were first introduced to Chi Kung through the practice of Tai Chi, some claiming to have been practising it for many, many years; in fact many Western

Tai Chi teachers also claim to teach Chi Kung as well, although it is not clear exactly what form of Chi Kung and to what level. It appears to be External Chi Kung or Wei Dan, using postures and external movement to drive the energy, increase its volume and develop strength; it does not appear to be comprehensive Nei Dan/Internal Chi Kung for inner cultivation.

CHI KUNG FOR HEALTH AND HEALING

Of the many applications of Chi Kung this may be the one that becomes most widely spread in the West. There are very few parallels and comparisons in effectiveness. However, it is important to appreciate the full range of what is meant by Chi Kung healing. Chi Kung is a general umbrella word for many different forms; for instance, acupuncture, the very wide-spread technique now firmly established throughout the West, can be considered a form of Chi Kung, as can acupressure.

However, as a distinct healing application there are two very separate and different approaches. The first is called 'Healing Exercises' which involve set exercises that you do yourself and which must be performed in a very exact way; there are many different kinds of these for many different conditions and symptoms. In regard to Chi Kung Healing Exercises I spoke to one Chinese teacher who said that she knew about fifty Chi Kungs, but that this was really nothing much, because her teacher in Beijing knew 400.

Indeed, in China today, people are developing new forms and applications of Chi Kung every day. Chinese Chi Kung medical books are full of these Healing Exercises and programmes that you can do yourself.

The second approach is what is known as 'Wei Chi/External Healing'; this is performed by a practitioner on a 'patient', and consists of exact sequences of hand movements and manipulations which are done in a very set way for specific medical conditions.

Wei Chi/External Healing is performed by a 'healer' on a 'patient'. This presupposes a comprehensive working knowledge of the meridian/energy system and the principles involved in Oriental diagnosis and treatment. They can constitute a series of 'formulas' and procedures for specific conditions, much as exist in 'formula acupuncture' – follow the instructions, and the problem is resolved. There are Chi Kung treatments for asthma, arthritis, sciatica, headaches, nervous system, motor system, digestive system, skeletal/muscular conditions and so on. Comprehensive listings can be found in the books of Chi Kung Healing which are now beginning to appear in the West.

Because of its close affiliation with acupuncture, and the ever-increasing number of acupuncturists, it is a fair prediction to say that in the near future many acupuncturists will begin to add the title 'Chi Kung Healer' to their business cards, as training for Chi Kung Healing becomes more widely available. Currently (1992) there is only one formal comprehensive training programme available in the United States, at SAMRA Oriental Medical College in Los Angeles, although there is no question that such programmes will increase.

In the Orient there has been something of a tradition that before you were allowed to study acupuncture you first had to become proficient in Chi Kung, for the rather obvious reason that if you did not know how to organize, move, purify and manipulate your own energy then you could hardly do that for somebody else.

The closest comparison to this in the West is 'Therapeutic Touch' – which can be considered a Western form of Chi Kung Healing and which will be described in detail later.

CHI KUNG AND SEX

Sex is one of the most compelling and perplexing aspects of life for people in the West. It generates excitement, confusion, passion, depression, love, compulsion, joy . . . Every human emotion is involved with sex, and yet we have very little understanding of it. One of the major problems in the West is that we do not understand or recognize it as being related to our energy system or our chi; include our energy system and suddenly everything can begin to make some more sense. Trying to understand sex without including our energy system is like going to a foreign country without speaking the language and with no map.

Sexual Chi Kung is well understood in the Oriental system – your sexual energy is associated with your primary motivating energy, your biological animal level of being, and is known as Jing. This is one of the Three Treasures – Jing, Chi and Shen. The retention and cultivation of Jing is considered to be essential in order to progress to higher levels of energy and spirit. Whether you are single and alone, married for many years or with a wild and passionate new lover, it is essential to understand and control your own Jing and know how to preserve it.

There are two aspects to sexuality – sole cultivation and dual cultivation. As implied, sole cultivation is done on your own, dual cultivation is done with a partner.

Sole Cultivation

The most important element in sole cultivation is not to lose or discharge your Jing, because it contains some of your most potent and powerful essential energy. For the man this is the sperm, and there are a series of exercises which strengthen a man's ability and power not to ejaculate even though engaged in full sexual arousal and contact. For the woman the Jing is contained in the ovum and the sexual secretions and fluids, and also in the blood that is lost monthly in menstruation; a woman learns various exercises to strengthen the sexual organs and tissues. The training is to learn how to take the energy of your own Jing, and perhaps later, a partner's, and to draw it up the Governor Channel in the middle of the back, to the higher centres.

Dual Cultivation

As implied, dual cultivation means sexuality with a partner. At its best sex is an act of love. Sex without love is like seasoning without the food; it may be hot and spicy, but it doesn't nourish you, and it can leave a funny taste. The most essential aspect of sex with a partner is that there is a very specific energy exchange that takes place; it is exchanged from each partner to the other and this serves to 'balance out' each one. This is perhaps the most compelling aspect of sexuality, and the aspect that drives people to it. The man has Yang Jing and the woman has Yin Jing, and in sexual contact these are exchanged. Dual cultivation involves developing the skill and abilities to control the interplay and exchange of sexual energy. In this way the sexual exchange between a couple can take place not just at the level of the Jing but also at the level of the Chi and the Shen (the soul and spirit levels) too.

Chi Kung allows for the development of sexuality from the primary biological level, through the emotional level to the cultivation of the spirit; this is a most valuable and important skill to learn. If these abilities are not developed then it is like letting fruit on the trees decay and rot, or not looking at and enjoying flowers in the garden; or it can lead to a compulsive constant search for new partners. Not only can it stop unnecessary confusion and pain, but it can also bring one of our greatest treasures into full fruition and provide us with the means to preserve and nourish that most desirable thing – our higher Love.

CHI KUNG FOR LONGEVITY

One of the most common archetypes generally held about China is that of the wise old sage, of whom it is impossible to tell the age. This is, in my experience, true. It is very difficult to know to the nearest decade how old some Chinese people are, especially when they are capable of taking on a half-dozen young bucks in a martial arts contest and throwing them all over the place. Close-up their skin has a golden glow, their eyes sparkle, their joints don't creak, their minds are crystal clear and the men father children in their seventies and eighties.

Contrast this with the West where in some instances people in their forties look as though they are in their sixties, their hearing is going, their minds are slipping and their physical strength is ebbing away. This will increase as the great bulging post-war baby boom greys, then turns white. Even the Rock'n'Roll rebel heroes are getting old.

Longevity is one of the great prizes in China. It means that you understood the Tao, and lived it. In China it is said that if you die at 120 years you die young. It is not a necessary thing to grow ill just because you grow old. It all depends on what you practise and cultivate. It depends on the quality and volume and purity of your essence, energy and spirit – your Jing, Chi and Shen.

There are many means employed to maintain health and achieve longevity – Chi Kung, acupuncture, herbs, diet, meditation, living 'in the Tao' – but the basic objective is the same: to keep your energy at its best.

One of the best ways to do this for yourself is through learning and practising Chi Kung on a regular basis. Do it every day. Make it part of your life, like brushing your teeth every morning. That is why millions of people in China do their exercises every day and the public parks and places are filled each morning with people doing slow, graceful, flowing movements to preserve and cultivate their energy – and thereby their Jing, Chi and Shen.

We are not talking here about theoretical niceties, or contrasting philosophical opinions and positions, we are talking about whether somebody lives in pain and discomfort, whether they can walk or whether they can even see or talk, whether or not they live the last years of their life getting multiple medical operations and whether they live in fear of losing their mind and their dignity. This is not just people you know, or your own parents, this may be you!

Except in the special case described below in the section on Immortality, each person gets older every day, and death is inevitable. However, it does not necessarily mean that you have to fall into decay. Practise Chi Kung and you will give yourself the best chance of a healthy longevity.

CHI KUNG AND EXTRA-ORDINARY HUMAN ABILITIES

It is well established and heavily documented throughout the history of the world that certain people have highly developed psychic and paranormal abilities. For children these are legends, myths, fairy stories, comic books and movies. For adults, they are the seers, sages, shamans, saints and medicine men and women. There are people who can do things for which there is no obvious explanation within our currently accepted laws of physics and science. This is the paranormal, beyond the normal, beyond the usually accepted abilities. Such people are able to do things which have no explanation. They have clairvoyance. They can foretell the future. They can heal at a distance.

This has become a source of intense enquiry in China lately. There have been investigations of extra-ordinary abilities by Chi Kung Masters (as there have also been similar investigations at universities and by scientific groups in the West).

In attempting to understand the mechanisms involved in extra-ordinary abilities, it is feasible to consider that it is based upon operating at a higher level than our normal sense perceptions and experience.

The problem arises when we have to take into account other ways-of-being and organizing our perceptions. One such example is that other peoples, in other cultures, experience space and time totally differently from us – Bushmen, Aborigines and Amazon tribes for example. In fact, they appear to be in a different universe from ours. The same state also occurs with mystics, shamans and medicine men and women who enter into altered states of consciousness, wherein they can by-pass normal time and space as we know it and 'all becomes one'; they can see the past and the future, know what someone else is thinking and feeling, and they can affect things at a distance. They step outside of the normal framework of time and space, and cause and effect, that we are usually familiar with and grounded in.

This is related to the inherent nature of our sensory apparatus. It is perfectly clear that there are only limited things we can perceive with our sense organs; the electromagnetic spectrum after all, is very large and we only perceive a tiny fragment of it – a very thin slice of the pizza indeed. Extra-ordinary human abilities are related to the ability of our sense organs and higher faculties to perceive at broader, higher and finer levels.

Through practice and cultivation it is possible to 'tune' our instrument (our sensory apparatus) to different frequencies than usual, hence the ability to do the extra-ordinary and paranormal. It seems that developing the higher functions of the pituitary and pineal glands is very involved in this process. It has recently been found by endocrinologists that both of those glands contain traces of magnetite, which is a component of compasses and also a major component of electromagnetic wave propagation. Advanced Chi Kung practice focuses on cultivating these two glands. Practitioners can perform all kinds of marvellous activities, including creating a 'Chi Field', a field of energy which can fill auditoriums or even sports stadiums. In the West we may be very familiar with this without knowing it – might Rock singers, charismatic performers and spell-binding politicians produce such chi fields without being aware of it? We all have the potential to develop these abilities. Advanced Chi Kung aids in such cultivation.

CHI KUNG AND SPIRITUAL DEVELOPMENT

Spiritual cultivation is part of all cultures, and every society has its own ways of approaching it. All cultures also protect their spiritual secrets, often kept esoteric and only made available and revealed to the carefully selected and initiated who must prove themselves worthy by passing certain tests that are designed to be difficult. If it was easy everyone would do it. In the Chi Kung system these esoteric practices are called 'Inner Alchemy'. These are considered to be higher level practices, which develop heightened states of being.

In order to protect the knowledge certain processes have been employed historically:

- One of these is not to write it down, so that it would not be found and misused.

- Another protection was that it was passed on verbally from teacher to student. One of the reasons that a teacher would periodically test a pupil was to see if they were worthy, to filter out anybody who was not ready or who was inappropriate. You would not want this knowledge in the possession of someone who used it solely for egocentric advantage and empowerment.

- A further means of protection was the use of symbolic and metaphorical language. Even if somebody did find one of the sacred texts, they wouldn't have any idea what it all meant, because they wouldn't know, for instance, what 'the Dragon and the Tiger uniting in the Inner Cauldron' meant.

If you ask an initiated practitioner any questions about this level of Chi Kung they may completely ignore you, answer an unrelated question you never even asked, suddenly be unable to understand simple English, tell an incomprehensible story about someone and his Ox, hit you over the head with a stool, laugh uncontrollably or talk about what a nice day it is. It is just not done in the East to ask such questions. You wait – sometimes for a decade or two.

Recently ancient texts have been translated into English for the first time; books have been published in simple understandable language on aspects of the 'Inner Alchemy'; Taoist teachers have begun to spread the word. Taoism is having a tremendous resurgence in China itself and is now, for the first time, spilling over into the rest of the world.

In the Taoist tradition there are considered to be three bodies – the physical body, the soul body and the spirit body. These are cultivated through specific practices. You raise your Energy-Body to a higher frequency and volume and thereby cultivate the spirit body.

Sometimes this happened spontaneously in meditation, as described in 'Yin Shih Tsu's Experimental Meditation for the Promotion of Health' written when the author was eighty-two years old:

> The 'central spot' vibrated again, and there seemed to be an electric shock which pulsed in an oblique oval circle from my left shoulder to my left leg, so violently that it shook my bed; when the vibration became more intense it stopped abruptly. Then I felt another vibration behind my brain, descending along the backbone to stop abruptly in the coccyx . . . Two oblique oval circuits, on the left and right sides of my body, showed that the four psychic channels – yin ch'iao, yang ch'iao, yin wei and yang wei, had joined up. Thus for the first time I understood the inter-relation of the eight psychic channels and the nervous system and realized that there was nothing fictitious and unaccountable in it at all.

Such meditation practice can cause involuntary and spontaneous movements. This is what the Taoist monks do for the development of spiritual cultivation in the monasteries, actual practices that refine their energy. They are cranking it up to higher volume and frequencies. That's why the saints and highly developed spiritual practitioners of many other cultures are often portrayed as surrounded by pure light, and have haloes – their bodies are operating at a higher level than the normal person and actually radiating photons. All such practitioners are involved in processes and practices which are designed to refine and purify their bodies, and thereby raise themselves to a higher level of energy functioning. They are cultivating their subtle energy bodies – the soul body and the spirit body. This is a very fundamental aspect of all spiritual training and development.

CHI KUNG AND IMMORTALITY

The pursuit of immortality is a theme of Chi Kung. It is rooted in the most ancient traditions of China, and goes back before what has become known as Taoism to the earliest Shamanistic tradition. There are descriptions of the Hsien, the universal beings who lived on sunlight, and travelled to the edges of the universe at will. Elaborate and fanciful descriptions abound in folk Taoism. Whether this is intended to represent just an idealized state of being, or to represent an actual state of the liberated spirit, is unknown. This has become deeply embedded in Chinese folklore and mythology, and to some degree represents the highest aspirations of the common people, similar to the saints in Christianity. It also represents the highest aspirations of some Chi Kung practitioners.

It is considered that the spirit can be liberated from the body, and can freely, and at will, roam through the various realms of the universe. It is believed that the individual spirit can retain its form and integrity, and that it can be forever liberated. It can also choose to return to be reborn, similar to Buddhist reincarnation. There are various levels of accomplishment here. The highest achievement that can be gained is complete liberation. However, there are lesser levels of accomplishment too, whereby integrity of the individual spirit after death can be maintained for limited amounts of time – such as ninety days – before it begins to lose its integrated form.

The actual procedure, which for obvious reasons is kept very secret, is involved with condensing the energy-body into a 'pearl'. This pearl is the condensed essence of what we are, the purified stuff of the universe that we each have inside us – which is the spark that we call 'life' – refined into a ball. The spirit can then be trained to leave or re-enter the body, while the physical body is in deep meditation. There are stories of 'adepts' leaving their bodies in deep meditation for extended periods of time, and although they do not eat or move they stay warm and alive. At some point, maybe after weeks or even months, the spirit returns and re-enters the body, the eyes open and the practitioner is present in current time. It is said that the pearl leaves and re-enters through the Chi Kung point called Bai Hui, at the top of the crown.

When it is time finally to leave forever, then the practitioner has complete control over the process, and can choose the exact time at which to depart. There is a particular internal energy sequence which shuts down the body functions sequentially, while condensing the spirit into the pearl. The pearl/spirit then leaves the body for good, and the physical body 'dies'.

A description in the *Seven Bamboo Tablets of the Cloudy Satchel* by Deng Ming Dao says

> . . . a flow of energy mightier than any other . . . was rushing upwards into the skull. Slowly, his body was passing into night. The arteries were pooling. The organs were stopping, drying up. The nerves were dulling. Every trace of life force was drawn upward. There, it was closed off. The body was in eclipse. The sun was contained in the head. The three selves became one, until in a

> powerful fusion, his soul launched itself away. The process took about twenty minutes.

This belief and practice has parallels with Tibetan, Buddhist, Christian and other spiritual traditions throughout the world. The mysteries of Life and Death may never be fully known to us, but the Taoists certainly have their own comprehensive version of it.

APPLICATIONS IN SUMMARY

The above is an overview of the general categories and applications of Chi Kung – for Fitness, Martial Arts, Health and Healing, Sex, Longevity, Extraordinary Human Abilities, Spiritual Development and Immortality. Each one is used for its own specific reasons, and each has its appropriate place. It's all a question of what is applicable and appropriate for who and when.

There are parallels to Chi Kung in all cultures, and definitely so here in the West – for instance ballet dancers have mastered 'anti-gravity' Chi Kung, even though they have never heard of it; heavyweight boxers have developed 'Iron Shirt Chi Kung' but don't call it that; priests purify and refine their 'energy body' by their everyday lifestyle; and young children enjoy 'Spontaneous Chi Kung' by stretching and bending and rolling and jumping . . . Exercise of all kinds is a form of Chi Kung – if you just add the energy meridian system into the picture.

Chi is an essential part of our being. The key to cultivating it is to find out what is appropriate and right for you, now, and take it from there. I hope this brief guided tour of the applications of Chi Kung has at least mapped out the general territory.

EXERCISE FOUR

Knocking at the Door of Life

Activate the deep level of your ancestral energy.

Purpose
An external, dynamic Wei Dan exercise to stimulate your deeper level

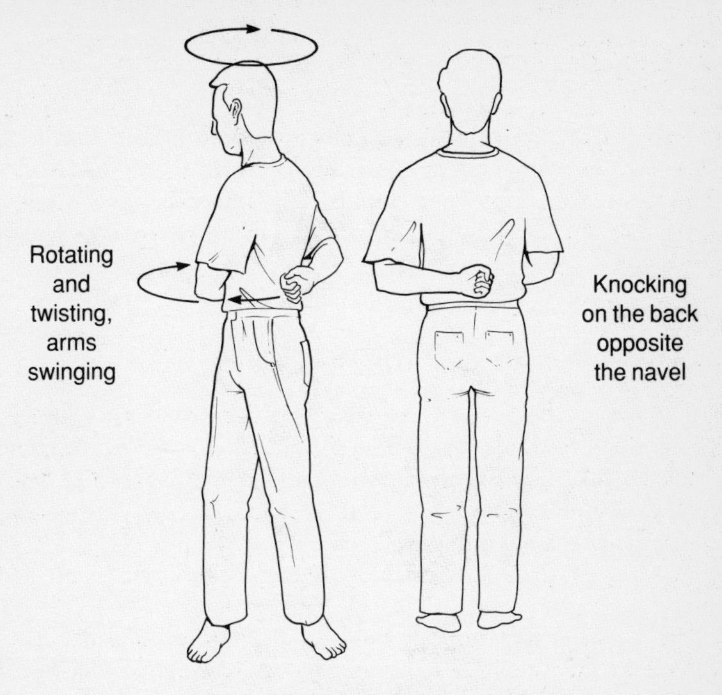

Fig. 17. Knocking at the Door of Life

of genetic energy, and to bring it into the two primary energy channels of the Governor meridian and Conception meridian, in order to feed it into all of the other energy meridians.

Sequence

1. Stand, with your feet shoulder-width apart. Let your arms hang down naturally by your sides. Clear your mind. Look with soft unfocused eyes into the mid-distance. Relax.

2. Slowly begin to turn from side to side, leading with your eyes, then your head, down to your shoulders and gradually into your pelvis. Let this swinging movement get bigger and faster until it is smooth and easy. Let your arms begin to swing loosely, following the turning motion of your shoulders.

3. Let the twisting motion slowly increase, with your elbows loose, fluid and flexible, so that your hands begin to slap on opposite sides of the torso at the level of your waist and navel.

4. In front, the palm of one hand softly slaps your waist on the left and right sides.

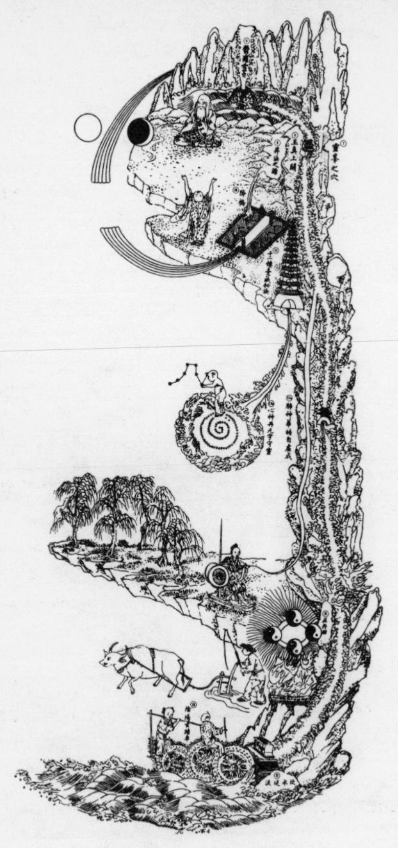

Fig. 18. Inner Alchemy
The Microcosmic Orbit
Circulating Chi in the Governor and Conception Meridians
Tang Dynasty Internal Body View 7–10th Century AD

5. On your back, as you reach the end of each swing, consciously direct the rear hand by bending your elbow slightly, so that the back of the hand softly hits at a point on the spine opposite your navel, between lumbar vertebrae two and three. This is a major Chi Kung and acupuncture point called The Door of Life/Ming Men. This point connects to the kidneys, and the energy stored in them, which is inherited from your parents. This energy is known as ancestral energy or Yuan Chi and is very refined. It can be considered your genetic energy. Through this practice it is drawn out from deep in the kidneys into the Governor Channel, which runs up the centre line in the middle of your back.

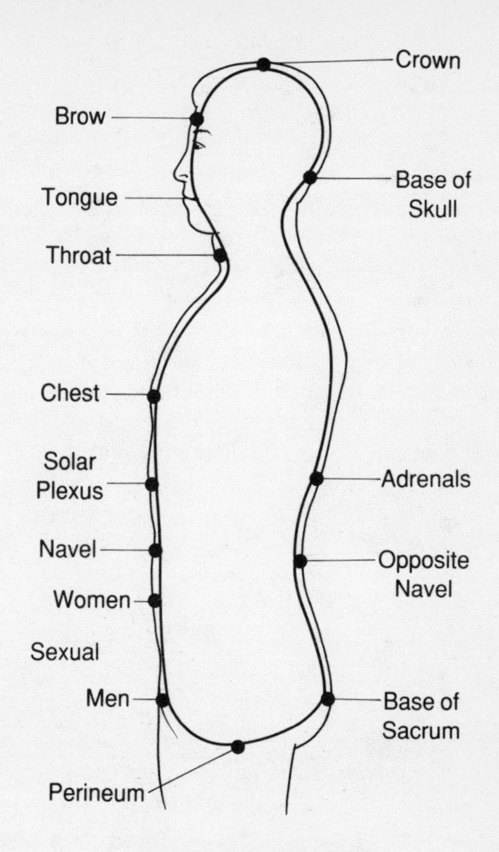

Fig. 19. Inner Alchemy
The Microcosmic Orbit
Circulating Chi in the Governor and Conception Meridians
Contemporary Internal Body View

7. Continue slowly and gently turning – and 'Knocking At The Door Of Life' – for as long as you wish or feel comfortable.

This exercise uses the simple momentum of rotating from side to side to stimulate your deeper resources of chi. As you hit the Ming Men point with the rear of your back hand you draw the ancestral energy/Yuan Chi into the major channel of the Governor meridian and thereby feed your deeper energy into all of the other meridians. This refined energy is drawn into the general energy circulation and acts as a catalyst to transform the energy of heaven (breathing) and earth (eating) which creates the essential energy/Ching Chi, and which then runs in the organ meridian system.

THE MICROCOSMIC ORBIT

This exercise is especially effective when the Governor Channel is linked up with the Conception Channel, in the procedure called The Microcosmic Orbit Meditation/The Small Heavenly Cycle/Xiao Jiu Tien. The Microcosmic Orbit is the foundation for all further internal practices, but the instructions are too extensive and complicated to describe in this book. There are numerous ways to do this practice. One approach is excellently presented in the books of Master Mantak Chia, which outline the procedure in detail: see *Awaken Healing Energy Through The Tao* and *Awakening Healing Light – Tao Energetic Medicine Of The Future* in the bibliography. However, the exercise is best learnt through personal instruction and guidance, and there is also an element of non-verbal transmission involved. Once you have the 'feel' for it from a teacher you can then go on to practise on your own.

5

How Does Chi Kung Relate to other Body-Energy Systems?

GIVEN ALL OF the above there is obviously a very wide range of possible applications of Chi Kung, each with its own merits and strengths, and its appropriate uses. It is so inclusive and comprehensive that it may seem that Chi Kung is all that you have to do; you may need no other practice. However, this knowledge has grown within the context of one culture only, that of China, and it is only one way of understanding how our energy works. The primary reason that we in the West have no tradition equivalent to Chi Kung is because we have had no model of energy equivalent to the meridian system.

But the meridian system is not the complete, or only, picture of energy in the body; other cultures have developed other systems which are parallel, but different, and have their own practices and traditions. In order more correctly to put Chi Kung into its proper perspective and context, culturally and historically – so that we are not hypnotized, seduced or mystified by its outward style – it is necessary to look at other Body-Energy Systems, compare it with them and consider its relationship to them.

We can find many equivalents and similarities to body-energy practices and manifestations in our own history and culture, although we are mostly unconscious of it in terms of how energy operates and works: we exercise, but don't call it Chi Kung; we do things to stay healthy, but don't call it Chi Kung; we observe people with remarkable powers and abilities, but don't call it Chi Kung.

SCIENTIFIC AND MEDICAL RESEARCH

Just because the energy system is not detectable to gross anatomy in no way means that it does not exist. Do TV and radio waves exist? Only when we have the means – the right instruments – with which to detect them. Up until recently there were not the right instruments to detect body-energy, so evidence was by necessity anecdotal and based upon reports by people who were especially sensitive. However, with the research conducted over the past thirty years in universities and laboratories in the United States, Russia, Germany, England, Japan, China and other countries around the world, it is now scientifically established. One only has to look at the work of Dr Robert Becker in his book *The Body-Electric*, Dr Richard Gerber in *Vibrational Medicine*, Dr David Eisenberg in *Encounters with Qi* in the USA, and the research of Dr Bjorn Nordenstrom in Sweden, Dr Hiroshi Motoyama in Japan and Dr Reinhard Voll in Germany.

This is such that nowadays there is a clear distinction made between the *Gross Anatomy* (the flesh, blood and bones that you can see and feel) and the *Energy Anatomy*. In the field of current research this has come to be called the *Subtle Anatomy*. This is the missing chapter of *Gray's Anatomy* – the anatomical Bible of Western medical science. Without it many things do not make sense (which is the reason that many people seek alternative treatments and get the results that they were unable to get from Western medicine). Include the Subtle Anatomy in the picture and suddenly everything begins to fit together into one coherent picture. The Energy-Body is the missing part of the anatomy. Energy medicine is the medicine of the future.

As we know, the universe outside of the range of our ordinary senses of seeing, hearing, touching, smelling and tasting is enormous. As human beings we come complete with the equipment to perceive the world around us, but within a very, very narrow range. However our minds are so powerful that we are now able to go far beyond our ordinary senses – from the micro to the macro – electron-microscopes to X-Ray telescopes. For the first time we can see deep into the structure and out to the ends of our universe. We now know, through the miracle of science, the electromagnetic spectrum. It may very well be that this is what the ancient Chinese called chi, or the Yogis called Prana, or whatever other culture gave it another name.

It is becoming clear that each cell in the body is an individual 'battery' which uses and stores energy. So, generating and accumulating energy is something we should all know about. All cultures have known this, to varying degrees, and this is what is embodied in the Body-Energy Models which each culture has developed.

There is now emerging a whole field of medicine based on what has come to be called Bio-electromagnetics; it is already extensively used all over the world every day – with TENS units, Sonar-grams, Electrotherapy, Magnetic Resonance Imaging equipment and so on, and yet the question is still asked if there is such a thing as energy in the body! The mind boggles.

CHI KUNG, OTHER BODY-ENERGY SYSTEMS AND THE ENERGY BODY

At this stage we need to take a step back and look at the larger cultural context. People all over the world, in all cultures and all times, have been aware of, and worked with, body-energy. It is one of the oldest forms of knowledge and science. Because it involves an understanding and wisdom which is based upon, and grounded in, one's own body and being, each person has had a laboratory and testing ground wherein it has been possible to experiment with energy – one's own. Now a person could find a nice quiet place and sit and meditate and become aware of how their energy feels, but it's about as likely that that one person could discover the deepest secrets of internal energy knowledge, as it is that the proverbial monkey could write this book, even if you gave it a word-processor complete with instruction manual . . . Hey! come to think of it . . .

CULTURAL BODY-ENERGY MODELS

In the broader context Chi Kung is only one way, out of a wide range of methods and techniques, of working with the Oriental Meridian System; however the Meridian System itself is only one of three major 'Cultural Body-Energy Models'.

There are different models of body-energy which have developed in different cultures, over the course of their history. These models are not all the same. They have grown up independent of each other, similar to the way that different cultures have developed separate languages and alphabets. This was especially so in historical periods when there was minimal geographical communication.

These three body-energy Models are separate and different, but overlap somewhat at the edges. It is similar to language: things that you can say in one language you cannot say in another; concepts you can have in one language don't exist in another; different languages can represent different ways of seeing the world, and of being in it. However, all languages describe the same basic human experiences.

The different models of body-energy are the result of the accumulated knowledge and wisdom of whole cultures, with the geniuses of generations – the most blessed, gifted and enlightened ones – adding their piece, until there was a generally agreed understanding of the anatomy and physiology of that model. The three Body-Energy Models developed independently and separately from each other in the three distinct geographical areas that we call the Orient, East-India and the West. They have become known and identified by the names:

- THE MERIDIAN SYSTEM
- THE CHAKRA SYSTEM
- THE AURA FIELD

Each of these consists of a complete body of knowledge, with its own paradigms and parameters. Each has its own complete and independent anatomy and physiology. Each is a separate system.

There is obviously a correspondence and relationship between the Chakras, the Aura Field and the Meridians. What the exact and particular correspondence is still remains to be examined and understood. There are differences of opinion about what the precise nature and functions of each model are, and no common agreement; but that's what happens when you keep things secret for a few thousand years.

However, these three 'Cultural Body-Energy Models' are the basic framework, the skeleton, by which body-energy functions. Also each of them is the basis and the ground for all kinds of different methods and techniques which have grown and developed over the centuries as ways to treat or affect body-energy. Before we can continue further it is necessary to outline and differentiate these different models and how they relate to each other.

A note for consideration: the following is the author's own

understanding of the three major Cultural Body-Energy Models as the components of the Energy-Body. This outline and thesis is not intended as a final conclusive statement, but as a stimulus to a way of thinking about, and approaching, this intriguing and important issue.

The Oriental Meridian System

The meridian system is the foundation of Chi Kung practice, but it is also the basis of Oriental medicine, martial arts and spiritual development. The meridian system has been established throughout the Orient; not just in China but also Korea, Japan, Vietnam, Cambodia, the Philippines and so on. This is as vast an area as the land mass of Russia and all of the European and Scandinavian countries. Each country and nation in the Orient, with their billions of peoples, has relied upon this foundation, knowledge and understanding of the meridian system, and each has interpreted it in its own way and contributed to its understanding.

The main features of the meridian system are:

1. There are twelve major meridians, each related to a particular organ.

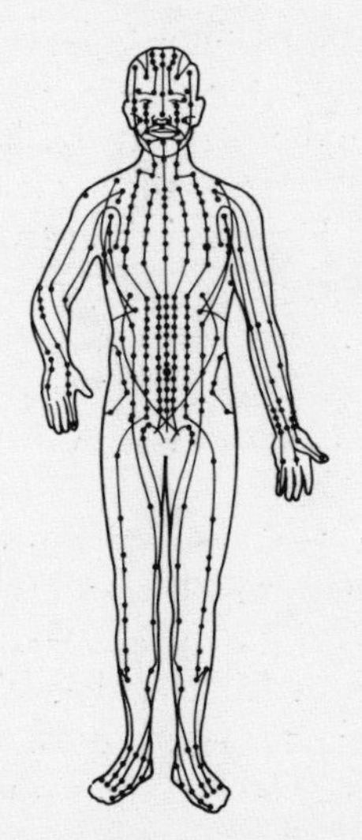

Fig. 20. The Meridian System

2. There are eight extra meridians which are reservoirs of energy.
3. The energy field which extends outside and around the body is called Wei Chi, but this is not finely differentiated.
4. There is a spectrum of relationships and correspondences between meridians, organs, tissues, sense organs, tissues, emotions and so on.
5. There are three 'levels' of energy – Jing, Chi and Shen.
6. There are three energy centres in the lower, middle and upper body.
7. Cultivation of the energy provides the foundation for development of the soul and spirit.

The meridian system is just one Body-Energy Model, with its own particular structure and function, and with a wide range of ways of affecting and treating it.

The Indian Chakra System

The Chakras are the central element and the main focus of Indian spiritual and religious traditions, such as Hinduism and Buddhism, and they are at the core of the practices of Yoga and Ayurveda. However, there is no uniformity of agreement about the anatomy of the Chakra system. Like the Taoists, the Yogis are known for their

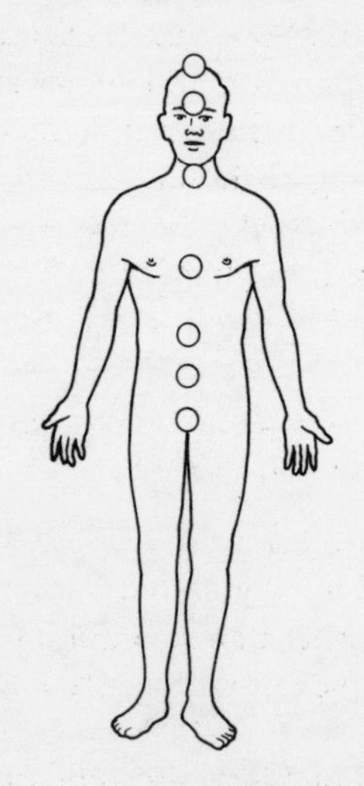

Fig.21. The Chakra System

extra-ordinary abilities and spiritual development which is primarily based upon a control of energy. In many ways Chi Kung and Yoga are equivalent. The following is an outline and illustration of the main features.

1. There are seven major Chakras.
2. Each Chakra has a name and a specific location.
3. There is an associated endocrine gland.
4. There is a related organ(s) and area of the body.
5. Each has emotional and psychological characteristics.
6. There is an ascending hierarchy of functions.
7. The Chakras relate to the Soul and the Spirit.

In addition to the central concept of the Chakras there are other major energy aspects of the Yoga system – the Kundalini and the Nadis and so on – but it is not relevant to pursue these here.

The Chakra system is at the foundation of Yoga practice, and the spiritual traditions of India. It is a separate, independent and self-contained Body-Energy Model, with its own range of methods and applications. Its use pre-dates recorded history.

The Western Aura Field

The Aura Field is the energy field which flows outside and around the body. This is highly developed in the Western esoteric tradition and is deeply integrated in the Indian model, although there is almost no correspondence in the Oriental meridian model.

The basic understanding of the Aura Field is that it is an energy field, or cocoon, around the body. There are many different opinions as to which layer actually does what, and why. This can be described in scientific terms as the bio-electromagnetic field which emanates from the central core.

In terms of the anatomy and physiology of the Aura there is basic common agreement about certain things:

1. There are seven different levels.
2. They are of increasingly higher and more refined frequencies.
3. They relate to each other in a series of harmonics.
4. Each field has a specific colour, which is reflective of its state of functioning.
5. They have an ascending hierarchical relationship to each other.
6. They interact with the Chakras.

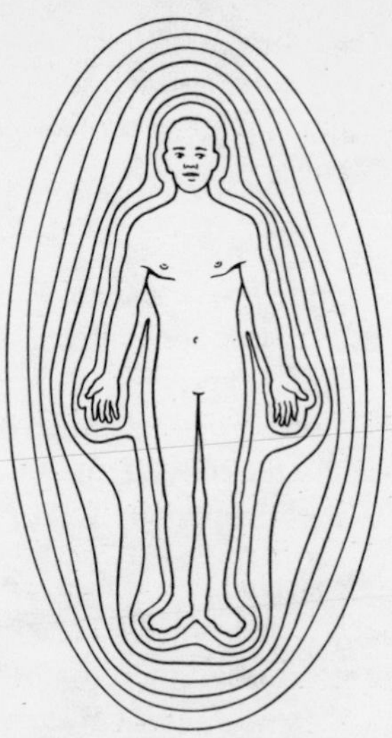

Fig. 22. The Aura Field

7. It is generally considered that the higher fields are related to what we describe as the soul and the spirit.

The Aura extends out around the body, like an antenna, and is the primary way through which external energies and influences are able to affect our bodies – from the earth's fluctuating magnetic field to electrical power-lines.

(One form of 'Aura cleansing' has been intuitively and mostly unknowingly practised all over the world by just about everybody – going for a nice walk in the park or countryside. Whether someone knows it or not, their Aura Field is cleansed by being in nature, and that is why we feel 're-freshed'.)

In summary it should be stated that the Aura is an independent Body-Energy Model which has its roots in the Indian Chakra system, but has reached very refined levels of differentiation and understanding in the esoteric traditions of the West.

THE ENERGY-BODY

Each of these three 'Cultural Body-Energy Models' developed independently, in the context of its own culture. Each is essentially complete, but none of them alone is the whole story. However, when you put them together – put the image of each one on clear

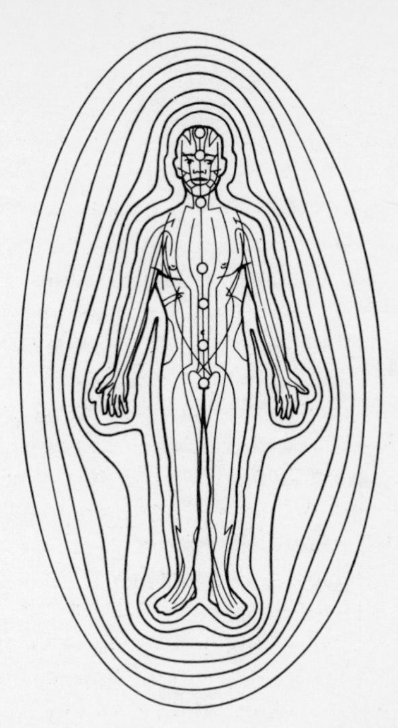

Fig. 23. The Combination of the Three Body-Energy Models to form the Energy-Body

acetate and overlay them – then *Hey Presto!*, you have the whole thing; the complete picture of The Energy-Body.

Perhaps now, in these days of open global communication, accessible information and scientific enquiry, we will finally begin to explain and understand the relationships and interactions between these three Cultural Body-Energy Models and how together they constitute The Energy-Body. This would be for the good of everybody, as having our energy-body healthy is clearly fundamental to everything else. It is the new definition of the state of health. It may represent the next step in the evolutionary development of humankind.

CONTEMPORARY ECLECTIC

In order to complete the picture, and bring us right up to date, it seems relevant to describe what is taking place now, in our contemporary culture.

In addition to the more traditional methods and techniques of working with body-energy described above, there has been a surge of new versions over the last few years. These have grown out of the Natural Medicine and Holistic Health movements, and have also appeared as a by-product of the enormous and amorphous grass roots movement, which suddenly appeared simultaneously around the world, dubbed 'The New Age' movement.

Some of these are simply new names on old systems, some are compiled from bits and pieces of other techniques, some of them have been created from first principles. Some are proprietary (an individual created it and gave it a name, and therefore stands to make their livelihood from it). The best and most appropriate title for this lot is perhaps 'Contemporary Eclectic'. It can include aspects of all of the systems and methods described earlier in this chapter.

Some of the names and titles which have recently appeared are: Energy Balancing, Biokinesiology, Psycho-Physical Therapies, Bio-Energetics, Core Energetics, Body-Centred Psychotherapy, Healing Touch, Touch For Health . . .

Some of it is excellent, some of it is not. It also depends greatly on the experience, skill and ability of the practitioner. Use your own judgement and intuition and your experience and response as the guide when trying any of these techniques.

However, there is one recent system which has grown here under strict scientific scrutiny, which in many ways is a Western equivalent of Chi Kung and is now accepted and integrated into Western medical science. Because of its significance in being already recognized and established in the medical context in the West this deserves special emphasis and elaboration. It is called Therapeutic Touch. Just as Chi Kung has been called 'Chinese Therapeutic Touch', Therapeutic Touch could be called 'Western Chi Kung'.

THERAPEUTIC TOUCH

Therapeutic Touch is both a medical science and a healing art. It is the name given to a vast variety of techniques of hands-on healing. It incorporates many ancient and modern methods of healing which involve passing energy/chi from a healer to a patient. These techniques cover a wide range, and include such methods as Aura Clearing, Centring, Chakra Balancing, Focusing, Healing Rituals, Trauma Release and many more. These and other methods are part of the Therapeutic Touch 'medicine bag', which continues to grow as individuals discover, create, develop and add new dimensions to this work as a result of their clinical experience.

As a recognized body of knowledge it was originally developed by Dolores Krieger, a professor of nursing, and her partner Dora Kunz. Through their clinical research and efforts it became accepted as an approved part of the curriculum of a fully accredited Master's degree programme at New York University. Currently Therapeutic Touch is taught to nurses at numerous Universities, Nursing Schools and private organizations in the US, and is now an approved modality by nurses for use in hospitals and other clinical settings. The title 'Nurse Healer' has come to be used for these practitioners.

Therapeutic Touch is effective, either alone or in conjunction with Chi Kung, acupuncture, medical treatment or other modalities, for a very wide range of conditions. These may be purely physical problems, emotionally based concerns, mental level issues or matters of spiritual development.

Another important aspect is that it is not limited to use in a professional context only; it is equally available to the lay-person. It can be learnt, and applied, by anybody who is prepared to undergo the necessary training. Everyone is a healer. Mothers can use it for their children; couples can do it to each other; friends can use it as a caring and giving activity together; you can even use it to take care of your pets. At the end of this book is an exercise of Therapeutic Touch for 'Generating Chi Between Your Hands For Healing'. Try it yourself!

Therapeutic Touch also has great benefits for the practitioners: it helps clear their own channels, increases energy sensitivity and helps cultivate the higher levels of practitioners so that they become more caring, more loving, more intuitive – in short they begin to operate and live from their higher levels. Learning TT is like moving up another rung of your own personal evolution.

Therapeutic Touch and Chi Kung Healing

Obviously TT has very great affinities with Chi Kung Healing. There are a lot of similarities in approach and technique; in fact they are reflections of each other. Both are scientifically approved medical modalities in their respective countries and therefore are the best candidates for clinical comparison. But while Chi Kung

Healers have a firmly established foundation of a model of anatomy and physiology in the Meridian System, Western Healers and Therapeutic Touch practitioners have developed more from an intuitive and experiential approach. However, Chi Kung Healers could most probably make perfect sense of the work of Therapeutic Touch practitioners, and vice versa. In China Chi Kung Healing is a major part of the curriculum of many traditional medical programmes, but as yet it is not much available in the West – although it's heading this way fast as Medical Chi Kung and Chi Kung Healing enter into the West.

At The Body-Energy Center, which I run with my wife Damaris Jarboux in Boulder, Colorado, the initial basics of Chi Kung meditation is a requirement for advanced levels of Therapeutic Touch training and the 'Body-Energy Practitioner' certification programme that we offer. We have found, through clinical experience, that including Chi Kung greatly enhances the effectiveness of Therapeutic Touch practice. It has also been found that integrating elements of Therapeutic Touch with acupuncture practice enhances the effectiveness of treatment, and acupuncturists are now beginning to train in this work and include it in their regular practice. In one sense this is ground-breaking work, while in another sense it is a classical tradition that has been taught in China for centuries – as 'Chi Kung Healing'.

SO THEREFORE . . .

In light of the foregoing – all the accumulated knowledge and experience regarding body-energy of all the world's major cultures and traditions – it is beyond question that the cultivation of one's Energy-Body is the foundation of spiritual development. It could well be that The Energy-Body is the anatomy and physiology of the Soul and the Spirit.

Of the major methods described above, Chi Kung is a complete system. It is something that you learn for yourself and once you have it, it is yours forever. However, this is not just an abstract idea, it is a set of practical techniques, methods and skills, which need to be learnt and cultivated, and integrated into one's life through practice. This is not something you just intellectually 'know'. It has to become part of your experience and your being. YOU HAVE TO *DO* IT!

EXERCISE FIVE

Energy Recharge

Use these postures to generate strength, and learn how to direct your own energy inside yourself.

Purpose
An external Wei Dan posture to increase the strength and volume of your chi, to develop concentration and to use the geometric form/pattern/configuration of the body in order to drive, focus and concentrate energy into the three major centres – the three Elixir Fields of cultivation.

The sequence
1. Stand in a calm, relaxed posture with feet facing forward parallel with each other, and shoulder-width apart, knees soft. Arms and hands hanging naturally relaxed by your sides. Empty your mind. Men face

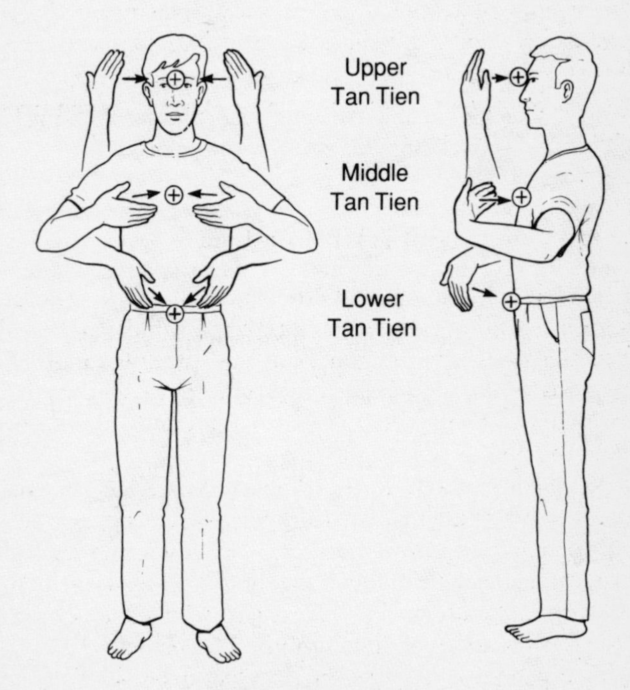

Fig. 24. Energy Recharge

towards the north. Women face to the south. If necessary this exercise may be performed sitting.

2. Using your mind open the point at the top of the crown – Meeting of the Hundred/Ba Hui – and let the chi from the heaven/sky enter into you.

3. Using your mind open the point at the soles of the feet – Bubbling Spring/Yong Quan – and let the chi from the earth/ground enter into you.

4. Using your mind draw the energy from the heaven down the back of your head and the back of your neck, and then draw the energy from the earth up the back of your legs through the back of your pelvis and along the centre line of your back (the Governor Channel) – to both meet at the point where the neck and the shoulders join. This point is called The Great Hammer/Da Zhui.

5. With your palms facing towards you, raise your hands in front of you with the fingers of one hand pointing towards the fingers of the other hand, 3 to 6 inches (7.5 to 15 cm) apart – as if you were holding a big ball in front of yourself. Your hands are now level with the centre of your chest with your palms facing towards you. Keep your elbows bent, soft and relaxed.

6. In this position the point in the centre of your palms – the Palace of Weariness/Lao Gong – is now level with the point between the breasts in the centre of your chest. This point in the palms is a very powerful point. It is the point used for healing and projecting energy out to other people, and it contains more chi than most of the other points. In this procedure you are using the power of this point to heal, strengthen and build yourself. You can use this point to direct and focus your energy to where you want it, as if it were the beam of a flashlight.

7. Using your mind, draw the energy from heaven and earth – which has been accumulated at the point at the bottom of the neck where the neck and shoulders meet – down through the arms and into the palms.

8. Standing in this position, 'focus' the energy radiating from the centre of the palms to the point on your chest – Within the Breast/Shan Zhong. This is the middle Elixir Field, a main centre of energy for your chest, and controls and influences the energy of your heart and lungs. Breathe slowly and evenly. Hold this position as long as you wish or are able to.

9. You have now created a posture where your own energy is in a feedback-loop between your palms and chest, and will begin to accumulate. You may feel it gradually growing more dense. The longer

you stand there the stronger it will get. Hold it for as long as it feels comfortable – and then a little longer.

10. Keeping your hands in the same posture bring them down until they are level with the point 2 inches (5 cm) below your navel – The Sea of Chi/Chi Hai. This is the lower Tan Tien and the lower Elixir Field. Hold this position as long as comfortable, then a little longer. Let your energy accumulate at this point. This point is the main centre of energy in your lower abdomen – it controls and influences all of the organs in the lower abdominal cavity and builds your essential energy.

11. Now, bring the position of your arms and hands back up level with your chest. Keeping the upper arms in the same position bend the forearms upward at the elbows at a 90 degree right-angle, so that your fingers are now facing upwards and your palms are facing towards your face. The point in the centre of your palms is now level with your eyes and your hands are slightly wider than the width of your head.

12. In this position use your mind to direct the energy beam from your palms to the point on your brow on the mid-line, between your eyes. Feel the chi accumulate. This point is called The Original Cavity of the Pure Spirit/Yin Tang. It relates to the pituitary gland, the brain and consciousness. It is the centre of the upper Elixir Field.

13. Hold this position as long as possible, and then a little longer. Feel the chi.

14. Bring your hands down and place them over the navel, left first and right on top for men, and right first then left on top for women. Breathe slowly and evenly. Pay attention to how you now feel. Find a word, image or symbol for how you feel and remember it.

Hold these postures for as long as you find comfortable. These positions can be held for an hour – or even longer. The longer that you do it the stronger the effect and benefit will be.

You have now completed a sequence which builds the volume and strength of your energy. It will refresh you very quickly when you feel tired. It can be equivalent to a day on the beach. It is like plugging yourself into the main electricity socket and re-charging. It will increase your strength and clarity immediately. Try it and see.

6

Chi Kung and You

HOW DO YOU DO IT?

THIS COMES TO the most important, central and crucial issue of all. **You have to do it**. This is not something that you are able to just know or talk or read about. It is not an intellectual activity. **You have to do it**. You have to sit or lie or stand and actually do the procedures. **You have to practise**. Only by actual practise is it possible to have the faintest idea what is being talked about here. Hopefully these words, on this piece of paper, will inform, educate, inspire and motivate you to find a teacher, book or tape, *and practise*. It is of no consequence or relevance to just know about it, without actually doing it. **Just do it!**

When you practise Chi Kung you will enter into a world of sensations and kinaesthetic awareness that you may not have been aware of before. It is like entering into a new way of being in yourself. Some of the sensations may be similar to others that you ordinarily have, while some may be completely outside of your previous experience. The sensitivity and subtlety increases with practice. At first you may notice nothing at all, but with continued practice you will develop sensitivity to, and an increasing awareness of, what is taking place.

The sensation of energy moving in your body can have many different forms:

- it can feel like flowing water
- it can be a tingling sensation
- it can appear as colour
- it can feel like weight – light or heavy
- it can feel like a warm current.

People feel it in different ways. This depends upon internal factors inherent in each particular person, just as some people tend to 'see' things in their mind's eye, while some 'hear' a dialogue, and others juggle abstract symbols and formulas. However, the way that you interpret or present it to yourself internally depends on your own internal communication system, and the way you do it best is what is right for you. So follow your own best feelings, sensations and instincts.

Through continued practice you will begin to cultivate stronger and clearer feelings and monitoring of your energy. Initially you are only able to get the faintest inkling, sometimes almost so faint that you don't really know if you are feeling anything at all. But with continued practice this tiny trickle becomes a stream which grows into a river which develops into an ocean of energy.

In the initial stages of practice and training you sometimes question if you are feeling anything at all and probably just go along on the conviction and strength of belief in the teacher. It is best to put yourself into the open-minded position of not questioning, but just doing what you are told. As a novice you should put your trust and confidence in your teacher and follow the instructions.

RECOMMENDATIONS AND PRECAUTIONS

One of the main reasons for secrecy in teaching is that while Chi Kung is enormously beneficial it is also potentially dangerous. If you do it wrong, there can be very serious consequences indeed, from not feeling well to life-threatening illness. This is one major reason the Chinese government is working to control it. It all depends on doing the practices correctly, which in turn depends on getting a good teacher. It is essential to find an experienced coach. It is also important at this point to mention some of the abnormal effects which can be experienced, and the problems, risks and precautions for anybody involved in practice. The Chinese call these Deviational Aberrations.

Precautions and contra-indications:

- Don't practise when you are emotionally upset.
- Don't practise if you are hungry or overfed.
- Don't practise if you are tired.

- Unless engaged in Dual Cultivation with a partner, don't practise after sex.
- Practise less and lighter during menstruation.
- Don't practise if you are ill or recovering from sickness.

Abnormal effects to be aware of:

On the physical level some of the sensations you can experience include dizziness, headache, shortage of breath or a feeling of suffocation, heartbeat acceleration, mouth dryness and scratchy throat, numbness in certain areas, abdominal distention, heaviness in the trunk and shoulders, an upward surge of energy from the lower abdomen, drowsiness and insomnia.

On the mental and emotional level abnormal effects include emotional instability, withdrawal, non-specific fear, anxiety, forgetfulness, being 'spaced out', losing concentration and other more extreme conditions.

To cultivate and develop good practice the following recommendations are made:

- Set time aside for yourself.
- Get good instruction.
- Understand the practices correctly.
- Get enough rest.
- Master the basic skills.
- Practise frequently and for long enough.
- Practise in a good, clean, fresh environment.
- Lead a balanced life with moderation.

CHOOSING A TEACHER

Chi Kung has many uses; it can be part of exercise, sports training, health care, meditation and more. Correspondingly, there are also various levels of teachers: some teach classical forms which have been carefully and precisely preserved through centuries and generations; some have been trained by highly accomplished teachers and initiated as hand-picked apprentices; some people have taken basic principles and mixed-and-matched their own combinations into their own 'style'; some people do not clearly understand what they are doing and consequently can be dangerous. For your own sake and safety, it is important to know the differences.

As there are no easily available 'authorities' to refer back to at this stage of development in the West, it is difficult for the beginner to know who is who, or what is what. One of the problems is the way in which this is discussed and described among practitioners themselves – it is similar to what takes place in many other non-verbal activities such as martial arts, painting, singing or dance. The language is inadequate to describe either the experience or the sensation. There is no easy, familiar or established vocabulary. However, there is an increasing variety of teachers of different levels of experience and accomplishment.

In choosing a teacher there is a clear intuitive 'knowing' – a definite understanding, insight or sense – that a teacher truly knows what they are doing. It usually correlates with a person seeming worthy of being a teacher, of deserving your respect, of being somebody that you feel you can 'entrust' yourself to in the same way that you 'entrust' yourself to a doctor or surgeon. It is to do with non-verbal things such as the look in somebody's eyes when they talk to you; the way in which they refer to themselves; the way that they move; the confidence and modesty with which they act; their sense of humour, kindness and gentleness; the way they physically touch you; whether they seem to be doing things for your best interest.

Also look at how they are themselves: are they an example of what they are speaking about? How are they in normal life? Do you regard them as a role model? How are their other students? How do other people feel about them?

These indications are not fanciful or vague. They are very real and palpable. They may be all that you have to go on. Listen to yourself clearly. Listen to your own responses, use your own intuition, instinct and judgement. Trust and follow them. They are right for you.

We are accustomed in the West to having, and expecting, certain attitudes, actions and responses from teachers. This is related to how we in the West view ourselves – our sense of individuality and personal identity. This is not the same in the East, where this sense of self is not necessarily shared – it is not that it is 'impersonal' so much as 'transpersonal'; we are so much more than our personalities and limited self identities. At the heart of some of the teaching and practices is a kind of dispassionate detachment. The teacher is not necessarily trying or wanting to be 'nice' to you or be liked by you. Their concern reaches to the transpersonal, higher level of you.

Individual Teachers' Attitude and Investment

It has to be clearly acknowledged and borne in mind that certain teachers have a very strong vested interest in promoting their own individual style and tradition. This is for a variety of reasons, some of which may seem valid and others not.

1. They sincerely believe in their own style, otherwise they would not do it.
2. This is, in some cases, their profession. They earn their income and provide for their family through teaching and have as much vested interest in retaining this as the basis of their livelihood as any other person does in any other profession.
3. If they taught somebody everything that they knew then a) they would stop coming to them and b) they would probably go and teach it themselves and set themselves up in direct competition.
4. Some teachers have a personal issue about being considered the Teacher/Master/Sifu, and therefore do not want their students to be at a level of equality with them, in order to retain their own relative position and authority.
5. A lot of the attitude of teachers is cultural in China. If somebody from the West trained or apprenticed directly under a Chinese teacher/master then they will also probably accept and adopt certain inherent, unconscious, deeply-rooted attitudes of that teacher, and therefore the cultural attitudes and mannerisms that underlie it. For example: they might wear Chinese clothes instead of a work-out suit; they may not encourage, or respond to, questioning in a way that is normally expected in the West; they might want you to use a particular word as a Chinese greeting or bow in a specific way. Such mannerisms may attract or alienate you, depending on your own inclination, however they are probably unconscious on the part of the teacher. If it feels OK, then go along with it.
6. Some of this knowledge is rightly deserving of utmost respect. The acquisition of it has been hard earned by practitioners who have committed their attention and devotion to their practice. It should not be taken lightly. The issue of respect for your teacher is of very great importance in the East. Your teacher is sometimes considered to be more important to you than your own biological father!

In choosing a teacher use your best judgement and come to your own conclusions.

WHAT HAPPENS IN PRACTICE?

The practice of Chi Kung goes in stages. Apart from the higher levels of spiritual development and immortality training in Inner Alchemy, practice can generally be described as following the progression – to cleanse, to generate, to increase, to accumulate, to refine, to circulate, to store, to preserve and to discharge your energy.

To Cleanse

The first thing is to cleanse yourself of any stale, impure, toxic and old chi. This is done through using the breath, as in The Six Healing Sounds, or using movements to shake off and discharge negative chi, or through using the mind to purify.

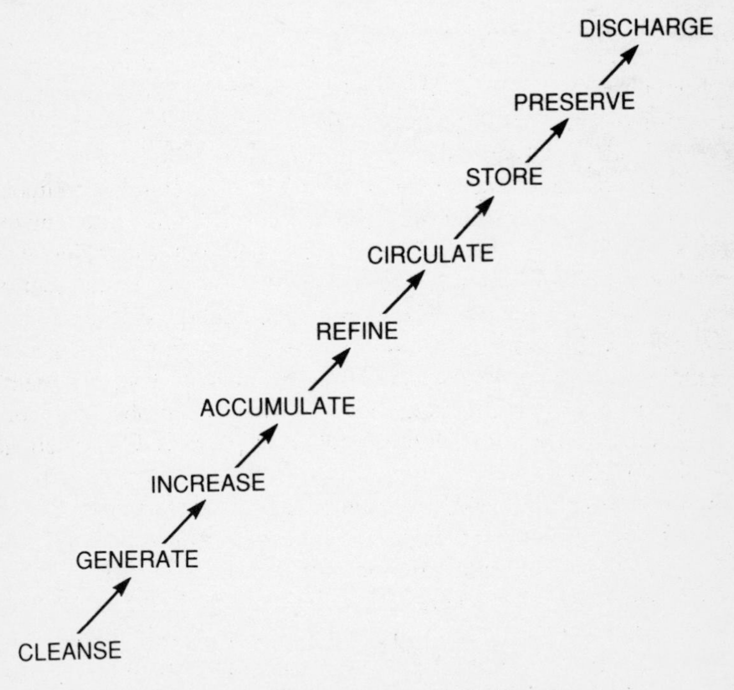

Fig. 25. The Ascending Progression of Chi Kung Practice

To Generate

The next step is to know how to focus your own energy. How to start it up. Where is the ON button? Well, there are a number of different ways, but one of the primary ones is to focus around your navel/umbilicus. This was where energy/food/nutrition/pre-natal chi originally came into your body. It is the safest, most secure and most stable place in your being – the Centre Place. It is Home-Base. Learning to put your attention and concentration there is one of the most important things.

To Increase

Increasing your chi is done through learning how to build it in your body. You take your own energy and learn to preserve it, so that it does not leak out and drain away, then you develop the ability to draw it in from the outside, as in absorbing it from the environment – for example sunshine, trees, moonlight. You also begin to live differently, eat better, sleep better, not get drained and exhausted, choose supportive people and situations.

To Accumulate

Accumulation of chi is developing the ability to build it up inside yourself, to increase your capacity to take a bigger charge, like a battery – some people can run little flash lights, some can start diesel engines on railway trains. The ability to take the maximum amount of energy is what is meant by accumulation. How much can you take in? This develops through practice. Just like weight-lifters – the more you do it the better you get, the more you practise the stronger you become.

To Refine

Once you have the energy internally developed, the next stage is to refine it. There are ways to purify it progressively. The twelve internal organs hold and store negative emotions. The practice of The Fusion of Five Elements works to purify the negative aspects of the emotions. The major emotions are:

Anger	(from the liver and gall bladder)
Joy	(from the heart, pericardium, small intestines and triple heater)
Sympathy	(from the spleen and stomach)
Grief	(from the lungs and colon) and
Fear	(from the kidneys and bladder)

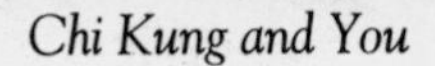

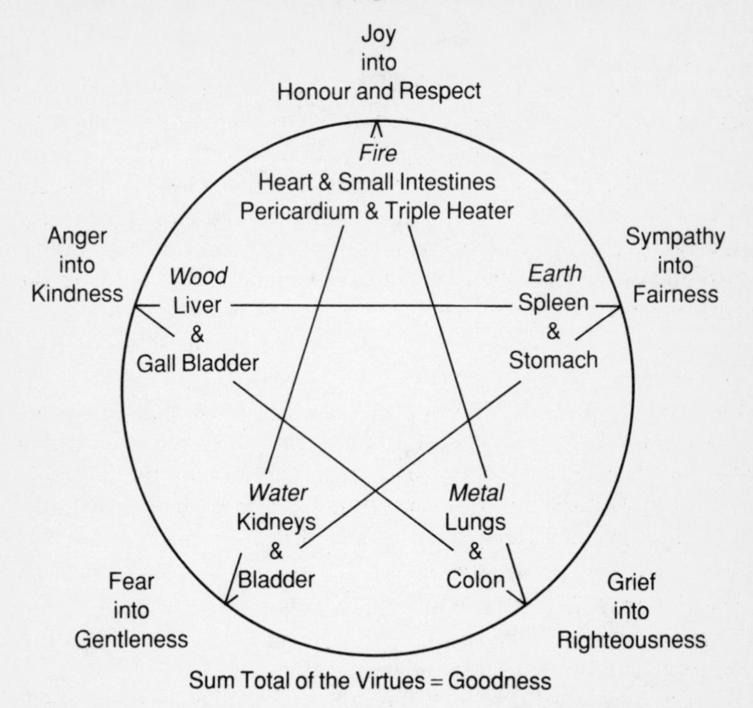

Fig. 26. The Transformation of Negative Emotions Through The Five Elements, and the Cultivation of the Virtues

The negative aspects of these emotions are broken down into their purified constituent components.

It then becomes possible to move beyond your emotions, and to cultivate The Virtues.

Gentleness	(in the kidneys and bladder)
Kindness	(in the liver and gall bladder)
Honour and Respect	(in the heart, pericardium, small intestines & triple heater)
Fairness	(in the spleen and stomach) and
Righteousness	(in the lungs and colon).

Combined together, these virtues constitute **Goodness**.

To Circulate

The refined chi is then circulated in the meridian system and the Elixir Fields. You practise the basic circulations of chi through the eight extra meridians and the twelve organ meridians. You thereby circulate throughout the whole meridian system, and out and beyond the body. Health is the free-flow of good chi, so that you circulate it freely. If it gets stuck in any one place then you are able to know it, and move it at will.

To Store

It then becomes possible to take this refined chi and store it, and pack it into the tissues and cells. You can hold more energy. Your cells each become better individual batteries which each hold more charge. You can put your energy into the bone marrow. You can store it in your fascia. You can absorb more energy. You become bigger and fuller and stronger. You become healthier.

To Preserve

You become able to preserve your own chi, to keep it fresh and clear. You develop strong filters which stop negative and unwanted chi from entering into you. You are able to protect yourself – from external influences like climate (windy, hot, dry, damp, cold), from negative emotions from other people (so that even if someone is negative towards you it doesn't get through). You are preserved in your own integrated field and it remains strong and pure.

To Discharge

When you have cultivated your own energy to its maximum you are then in a position to be able to discharge it as you wish, to pass it on and give it to other people in order to heal or positively affect them. This is known as Fa Jing. It can be done at great distances. You can create Chi-Fields in a room. It can be done in wondrous and seemingly unbelievable ways. This is the basis of Chi Kung Healing.

These abilities and skills develop slowly, through regular and consistent practice. But to 'Get It' you have to 'Do It'. So, do it!

After you have developed these capacities and abilities you are then able to get some of them to happen automatically, as if of their own accord. The more developed you are then the easier it becomes. It can get to a stage where the basic levels just happen by themselves and you can then concentrate on the higher practices and subtleties.

For instance:

- You can reach a stage where you just touch your tongue to the roof of your mouth in order to get the Microcosmic Orbit circulating.
- You can put yourself into automatic recharge when you go to sleep, and wake up fully refreshed.
- You can meditate and circulate your chi, and get the equivalent of a whole night's sleep.
- You can reduce the amount of food you need, and draw upon the more refined natural energy of nature (imagine what this would save you personally – and for the earth in total – if everyone could reduce their need for consumption).
- You can get control of your desires and needs, so that what you previously considered 'needs' become options that you may or may not choose to follow up on.
- You operate at a more refined and purer level of yourself, cultivating your soul and spirit level rather than being unconsciously driven and controlled by your emotions and desires.
- You operate from a better you.

And it can all start to happen automatically, just by taking the time to learn the practices and doing them regularly.

CULTIVATING YOUR ENERGY

As the energy grows you will develop a distinct and very clear sense of what it is. You will become clear about what your energy actually feels like when you move and direct it; there will be no question. It will be like standing in a shower, or having the wind blow on your body, or feeling the heat of the sun. You will be able to tell if your energy is flowing right, correctly and in which direction. You will begin to be able to direct it with your mind, and turn it on and off, speed it up and slow it down.

You will learn that you can't push it beyond a certain point, that you cannot make it go faster than it wants to or is able to. You will learn that it has its own distinct speed and integrity. You can't force nature any more than you can force a tree to grow or a flower to open. This cultivates a sense of respect for your own physiology and slows down the mind, as it has to wait for the chi. Anybody who has taken a young child or a puppy dog for a walk will be familiar with this feeling. It cultivates patience and respect for yourself.

Eventually you will begin to be able to 'read' the total overall state of your energy – when you feel strong, when you are at a low ebb, when you feel weak, when you are all 'lit up', and when you are ready to take on the world.

You therefore become familiar with what it feels like to have your energy good and strong and working properly. This may be a previously unknown and unfamiliar sensation; it is not the same as being on vacation, or climbing a mountain peak or skiing or whatever. It is a separate and distinct feeling-state which you come to recognize as being when your energy is good, clearest, strongest and at its best.

Finally, you can develop the ability to draw energy from the external natural world – sunshine, trees, grass, nature, mountains, lightning storms, waterfalls . . . All of the natural phenomena becomes available for you to take traces from and draw inside yourself. Even the moon, stars and other celestial forces become available to you to draw upon, and into yourself.

The key to all of this is practice. You have to do it, and make it

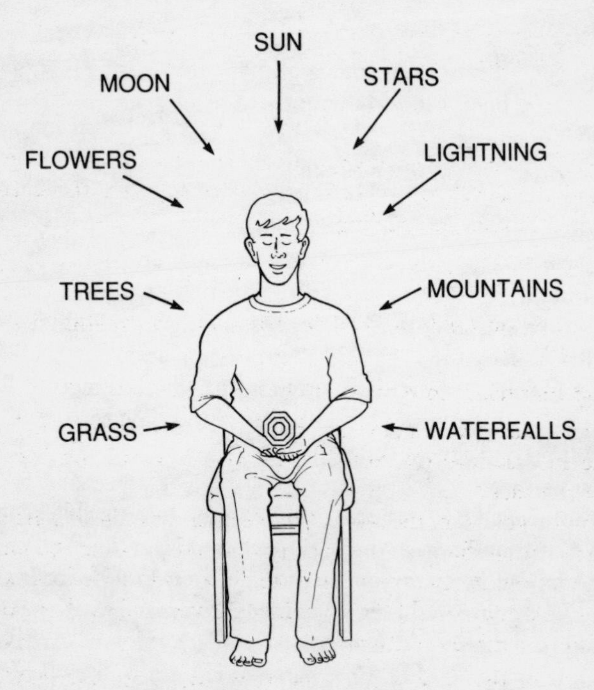

Fig. 27. Drawing Chi From Outside

part of your life. This invaluable treasure, your energy, is the essence of life, and is available to everyone. All you have to do is learn it and do it and you will take yourself to a new level.

Begin Chi Kung and you will begin Cultivating Energy. Practise Chi Kung and you will take the next step in your own Personal Cultivation.

- Do it good.
- Have fun.
- Be healthy.
- Cultivate yourself.
- Good luck.
- Stay in the Tao.
- . . . and may the Chi be with you!

EXERCISE SIX

Healing Energy in Your Hands

How to generate and accumulate your own energy and use it to heal yourself and others.

Purpose
External cultivation of energy for direct experience of one's own energy field and the development of one's own energy for transmission to oneself, or another, for healing.

The sequence
1. Sit quietly, feet flat on the floor, palms resting on knees, clear your mind and relax.

2. Clasp your hands in your lap, right over left.

3. Open your crown point at the top of your head, and as you breathe in draw the chi from the heaven down to the base of the neck at the back.

Open the points on the soles of the feet, and as you breathe in draw the earth chi up the legs, the back of the pelvis and up the middle of the back to join the heavenly chi at the base and back of the neck.

Using your mind, hold the combined heaven and earth energy here – the Great Hammer/Da Zhui point.

4. Close your eyes, concentrate your attention, empty your mind. Open your hands so that your palms are facing towards each other 3 to 6

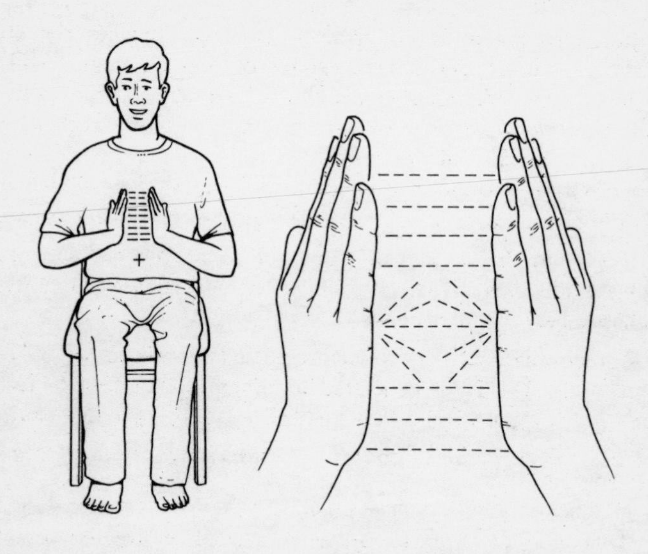

Fig. 28. Healing Hands

inches (7.5 to 15 cm) apart. Using your mind, draw the chi from the Great Hammer point at the base of the neck down into your palms. Pay attention to, and be aware of, any sensation that you feel between your hands. There can be a slight tingling sensation, or a feeling of warmth, or an electrical sense or some similar sensation. Pay attention to it and be as fully aware of it as possible.

5. Let this sensation begin to build. Let it accumulate. In this position your hands are creating a 'feedback' between themselves, and the physical energy/chi is beginning to increase.

6. As the chi increases, you will begin to be able to feel it more. Move your hands slightly towards and away from each other. Hold one hand still and move the other backwards and forwards and see what you feel. Switch hands. Play with the energy between your hands. It is subtle and refined. Do it gently and sensitively.

7. The chi is beginning to increase between your hands. As it increases it will feel 'fuller', as if there was actually something solid between your hands. In order to sense this, move your hands slightly closer together, then slightly further apart, let them bounce a little, as if

there are sensitive springs in your elbows which are responsive to slight changes in pressure and density. The energy is elastic, like rubber, and if you compress it, it will bounce back. Take your time developing this sensation.

8. Just keep holding your hands in this position and the chi will continue to build and increase, and as it does so, then it will begin to grow bigger. As your hands become sensitive and responsive to these subtle changes they will slowly begin to move further apart as the size of the 'chi ball' between your hands increases. It will also grow more dense. Move your hands closer together, and you will feel greater density, to the extent that it may take effort to get them closer.

9. If you do this in a very dimly lit room, against a white wall background, it is actually possible to begin to see the energy/chi exchange between your hands.

10. You now have a ball of concentrated and condensed energy between your hands. You have generated it from the energy of heaven and earth and your own life energy by performing a simple manoeuvre and practice which everybody can do. You can now use it in whichever way you want.

Use it on yourself: for instance bring it to a knee or ankle by placing your hands either side of the area that you want to treat so that the energy flows between your hands into, and through, the area; bring both hands side-by-side to direct it to a particular area such as an aching waist or an upset stomach; bring it to your eyes, or ears, or to help relieve a headache. You can use it in whatever way you want or need to.

(The familiar posture, seen in all cultures around the world, of lying, relaxing, with hands behind the head, is an instinctive Chi Kung position. The energy from the palms is directed to the energy point at the base of the skull – the Jade Pillow – which feeds into, and thereby relaxes the lower brain which is responsible for many automatic regulatory functions in the body such as temperature, heart rate, respiration and so on.)

Use it to help a child, or loved one or a friend. Take this energy and place your hands either side of an area that hurts, for example an aching shoulder, an injury, post-surgical recovery, whatever hurts or is in discomfort.

Use it to treat a pet, a sick plant, your goldfish, the flowers.

This exercise outlines the basic technique for generating your own energy to use in whatever way you want. Try it and see. People have been doing this throughout time, because it is natural and it works.

There are many uses of this healing energy in your hands. It is not a substitute for professional medical advice or treatment, but it is using one of the basic gifts which we are all born with, and which was the very earliest foundation of the art of healing – the art of touch. One final ingredient that has been found to increase the effectiveness – add Love.

Summary of Exercises

THE SIX EXERCISES in this book are each independent and self-sufficient. They have been selected and designed to be able to be done by anybody in average health. They can each be done in the way and for the purposes specified. However, they are also developmental and accumulative. If you start at the first one, and progress through in sequence, they form a whole which will increase the effectiveness of each one.

Some points to keep in mind while practising:

- To begin, do it slowly and gently so that you get the hang of it.
- These exercises are general guidelines. Don't get stuck on following a rigid form.
- Understand the basic principles and develop it from there, using common sense.
- Experiment – within these guidelines.
- If it doesn't feel right, or you get unexpected responses, then discontinue it, or slow down and don't do it so hard or so long.
- If in doubt bring your chi to your navel.
- Make it part of your life.
- Try again, till you feel it is right.
- Do it until you get the flow of your chi.
- Practise, practise, practise, then practise again.

Your energy is the essence of your life. It underlies how you feel and how you experience yourself. It is yout *sparkle*. It is the foundation of your soul and spirit.

Your energy already belongs to you – it is available to you right now, if you want it. All you have to do is practise and not only will you develop a stronger, healthier body and a peaceful mind – it will also improve the quality of your whole being. It will greatly benefit you in both the present and the future.

- Chi Kung is the Instruction Manual of your energy.
- Chi Kung shows you how to turn your energy ON!
- Chi Kung means 'Cultivating Energy'.

Practise Chi Kung and you will cultivate your personal energy.

Practise Chi Kung and you will cultivate the quality and essence of your life.

Practise!

Bibliography

CHI KUNG

Berk, William R. *Chinese Healing Arts – Internal Kung-Fu*, Unique Publications, 1986.

Chang, Edward C. *Knocking At The Gate Of Life And Other Healing Exercises From China*, Rodale Press, 1985.

Chang, Stephen T. *The Complete System of Self-Healing – Internal Exercises*, Tao Publishing, 1986.

The Tao Of Sexology, Tao Publishing, 1986.

Chia, Mantak. *Awaken Healing Energy Through The Tao*, Aurora Press, 1983.

Taoist Secrets Of Love – Cultivating Male Sexual Energy, Aurora Press, 1984.

Books published by Healing Tao Books:

Transform Stress Into Vitality, 1985.

Chi Self-Massage, 1986.

Healing Love Through The Tao – Cultivating Female Sexual Energy, 1986.

Iron Shirt Chi Kung, 1986.

Bone Marrow Nei Kung, 1989.

Fusion Of The Five Elements I, 1989.

Awakening Healing Light – Tao Energetic Medicine Of The Future, 1993.

Connor, Danny with Tse, Michael, *Qigong*, Stanley Paul & Co. Ltd, 1992.

Deng, Ming-Dao. 'Chronicles Of Tao' Trilogy –

The Wandering Taoist, 1983.

Gateway To A Vast World, 1989.

Seven Bamboo Tablets Of The Cloudy Satchel. 1987.

All published by Harper And Row.

Scholar Warrior, HarperCollins, 1990.

Dong, Paul & Esser, Aristide H. *Chi Gong*, Paragon House, 1990.
Hu, Bin. *Keep Fit The Chinese Way*, Foreign Languages Press, Beijing, 1991.
Jahnke, Roger. *The Most Profound Medicine*, Health Action Publishing, 1988.
The Self-Applied Health Enhancement Methods, Health Action Publishing, 1989.
Jiao, Guo Rui. *Qigong Essentials For Health Promotion*, China Today Press, 1990.
Laing, Shou-Yu. *Laingong Shr Ba Fa – Therapeutic Chi Kung*, Chinese National Chi Kung Institute, 1988.
Li, Ding. *Meridian Qigong*, Foreign Languages Press, Beijing, 1988.
Taiji Qigong, Foreign Languages Press, Beijing, 1988.
Lu, K'uan Yu (Charles Luk). *Taoist Yoga – Alchemy & Immortality*, Samuel Weiser, Inc., 1984.
The Secrets Of Chinese Meditation, Samuel Weiser, Inc., 1984.
Montaigue, Erle. *Self Healing – Chinese Exercises For Health And Longevity*, Boobook Publications, 1986.
Ni, Hua-Ching, *Tao, The Subtle Universal Law*, 1979.
Workbook for Spiritual Development, 1984.
plus many other titles. Published by Union of Tao and Man.
Reid, Daniel P. *The Tao Of Health, Sex & Longevity*, Simon & Schuster Ltd, 1989.
Shih, Tzu Kuo. *The Swimming Dragon*, Station Hill Press, 1989.
Yan Xin. *Yan Xin Qigong And The Contemporary Sciences*, International Yan Xin Qigong Association, 1991.
Yang, Jwing- Ming. *Chi Kung – Health & Martial Arts*. 1985.
The Eight Pieces Of Brocade, 1988.
Roots of Chinese Chi Kung, 1989.
Muscle/Tendon Changing and Marrow/Brain Washing Chi Kung, 1989.
All published by YMAA Publication Center.
Zeng, Qingnan. *Believe It Or Not – Ancient And Mysterious Chinese Qigong*, Foreign Languages Press, Beijing, 1991.
Zhang, Enqin. *Chinese Qigong*, Publishing House of Shanghai College Of Traditional Chinese Medicine, 1990.
Zhang, Mingwu. *Chinese Qigong Therapy*, Shandong Science And Technology Press, 1985.

ORIENTAL PHILOSOPHY AND HISTORY

Cleary, Thomas. *The Inner Teachings Of Taoism*, Shambala, 1986.
Understanding Reality, University Of Hawaii Press, 1987.
Immortal Sisters – Secrets Of Taoist Women, Shambala, 1989.
Vitality, Energy, Spirit – A Taoist Sourcebook, Shambala, 1991.

Cooper, J.C. *Chinese Alchemy – The Taoist Quest For Immortality*, Sterling Publishing Co, 1990.
Crompton, Paul. *The Elements of Tai Chi*, Element Books, 1990.
Eisenberg, David. *Encounters With Qi – Exploring Chinese Medicine*, W.W. Norton & Co., 1985.
Legge, James. *The I Ching – The Book Of Changes*, Dover Publications, 1963.
Mitchell, Stephen. *Tao Te Ching*, HarperCollins, 1988.
Needham, Joseph. *Science & Civilisation In China*, Cambridge University Press, 1954.
O'Brien, Joanne with Ho, Kwok Man. *The Elements of Feng Shui*, Element Books, 1991.
Palmer, Martin. *The Elements of Taoism*, Element Books, 1991.
Scott, David & Doubleday, Tony. *The Elements of Zen*, Element Books, 1992.
Vieth, Ilza. *The Yellow Emperor's Classic Of Internal Medicine*, University Of California Press, 1966.
Wilhelm, Richard. *The I Ching or Book Of Changes*, Princeton University Press, 1950.
Wong, Eva. *Seven Taoist Masters*, Shambala, 1990.
Wu, John C. H. *Lao Tzu – Tao Teh Ching*, St. John's University Press, 1961.

ACUPUNCTURE AND ORIENTAL MEDICINE

Bensky, Dan & O'Connor, John. *Acupuncture – A Comprehensive Text*, Eastland Press, 1981.
Compilation. *Essentials Of Chinese Acupuncture*, Foreign Languages Press, Beijing, 1980.
Kaptchuk, Ted. *The Web That Has No Weaver*, Congdon & Weed, 1983.
Mann, Felix. *The Meridians Of Acupuncture*, William Heinemann, 1964.
Ross, Jeremy. *Zang Fu – The Organ Systems Of Traditional Chinese Medicine*, Churchill Livingstone, 1984.
Woollerton, Henry and Mclean, Colleen J. *Acupuncture Energy in Health And Disease*, Thorsons, 1979.
Worsley, J.R. *Traditional Chinese Acupuncture – Vol. I. Meridians and Points*, Element Books, 1982.
Traditional Acupuncture – Vol. II. Traditional Diagnosis, The College Of Traditional Chinese Acupuncture, U.K., 1990.

RELATED SOURCES

Bailey, Alice A. *Esoteric Healing – Vol.IV.*, Lucis Press, 1953.

Becker, Robert O. and Selden, Gary, *The Body Electric – Electromagnetism And The Foundations Of Life*, Quill, William Morrow, 1985.
Blavatsky, H.P. *The Secret Doctrine*, The Theosophical Publishing House, 1966.
Gerber, Richard. *Vibrational Medicine*, Bear & Company, 1988.
Goldman, Jonathan. *Healing Sounds – The Power Of Harmonics*, Element Books, 1992.
Krieger, Dolores. *The Therapeutic Touch*, Prentlce Hall, 1979.
Living The Therapeutic Touch, Dodd, Mead & Co., 1987.
Leonard, George. *The Silent Pulse*, E.P. Dutton, 1978.
Mastery, E.P. Dutton, 1991.
Mann, John and Short, Lar. *The Body Of Light*, Globe Press Books, 1990.
Tansley, David V. *Subtle Body – Essence And Shadow*, Thames and Hudson, 1977.

Glossary

ANATOMY

Acupoints: energy points on the surface of the body.

Meridian system: the pathway of thirty-five energy lines according to the Oriental tradition, including the twelve organ meridians, the eight extra meridians and related subsidiary pathways.

Microcosmic Orbit / Small Heavenly Circuit: the circulation of energy along the Governor and Conception meridians.

Mo: Meridian, Channel, Vessel, Energy pathway.

Pa Kua: The eight-sided figure/octagon.

The Eight Extra/Miraculous/Psychic Meridians: the meridians which function as reservoirs of energy. Governor (Du Mo), Conception (Ren Mo), Thrusting (Chong Mo), Girdle (Dai Mo), Arm and Leg Linking and Connecting (Yang Ch'iao Mo, Yin Ch'iao Mo, Yang Wei Mo, Yin Wei Mo).

Three Chou: the areas of the upper, middle and lower abdomen.

Three Elixir Fields/Three Fields of Cultivation/Three Tan T'ien: centres of energy in the lower abdomen, mid-torso and head.

Three Treasures: the Jing, Chi and Shen.

Triple Heater: one of the twelve meridians/officials which controls temperature, amongst other functions.

Twelve Organ Meridians: the aspect of the meridian system related to each of the twelve major organs/officials.

LAWS AND PRINCIPLES

Eight Principles: a way of describing energy in terms of its basic polarities – yin/yang, interior/exterior, excess/deficiency, hot/cold.

Table of Correspondences: the correlations of things assigned to each of the Five Elements.
Taoism: the philosophy/religion which espouses The Tao.
The Five Elements: a system for classifying nature in terms of its essential characteristics – Wood, Fire, Earth, Metal and Water.
The Tao: The Way of nature.
Yin & Yang: the primary polarity of natural phenomena.

CHI

Shen: the spirit.
Ta Chi, Ku Chi, Wei Chi, Yuan Chi, Ching Chi, Hsien-T'ien Chi, Jing Chi: various manifestations of internal energy in the body.
Wei Chi: external healing
Yang Jing: Male primary sexual energy.
Yin Jing: Female primary sexual energy.

CHI KUNG

Chi Kung Healer: a person who uses Chi Kung to heal.
Dao Yin, Tu Na, Tugu Naxin: older names for what is now known as Chi Kung.
Dynamic, External, Wei Dan: postures and movements of Chi Kung.
Fa Jing: energy projected out of the body by a Chi Kung healer.
Medical Chi Kung: the application of Chi Kung by a healer for medical reasons.
Qi Gong, Qigong, Chi Gung: alternative spellings of Chi Kung.
Quiescent Chi Kung: preparatory practice to calm and clear oneself.
Shaolin: a temple famous for its Martial Arts Chi Kung.
Static, Internal, Nei Dan: meditation and mental control of Chi Kung.

CHI KUNG FORMS

Inner Alchemy: the spiritual tradition and training.
Sole cultivation and Dual cultivation: sexual practice to preserve the Jing.
Tai Chi Chuan: a movement form used for martial arts or health conditioning, of which there are numerous variations and schools.
Various forms, styles, formulas and sets: which have been developed, including The Five Animal Frolics, The Eight Pieces of Brocade (and its many variations), The Six Healing Sounds, Bone Marrow Washing, Hard Chi Kung, Iron Shirt, Muscle and Tendon Changing, LuLu Dao Yin, Spontaneous Chi Kung, Fusion of Five Elements, Tai Chi Chi Kung, Swimming Dragon, Wild Goose, Flying Crane.

PROPER NAMES

Ching: Book/Classic
Hsien: a realized and enlightened person
I Ching: The Book of Changes.
Nei Ching: Huang Ti Nei Ching/The Yellow Emperor's Classic of Internal Medicine.
Tao Te Ching: the first classic of Taoism, said to have been written by Lao Tzu.
The Eight Immortals: the saints/archetypes of Folk Taoism.

PHILOSOPHY

Adept: same as Master.
Buddhism: an Eastern philosophy/religion which follows the tenets of Buddha.
Master: a person who has had this title conferred by his/her Teacher/Master, showing that they have reached the highest levels of achievement in a particular practice.
Shaman: a priest or practitioner who can control and influence events in both the material and spirit worlds.
Sifu: Teacher.
Wu Wei: non-action, non-interference, the path of least resistance.

MEDICINE

Acupuncture: the insertion of hair-fine needles, and the burning of a plant leaf called Moxa, on acupoints to effect the meridian energy. There are many different forms and styles of acupuncture – Classical, Traditional, Formula, Electro and so on.
Pulses: six locations on each wrist, totalling twelve in all, which inform a practitioner about the state and condition of the twelve major organs/officials.
TCM / Traditional Chinese Medicine: the title given by the Communist Government in the People's Republic of China to describe their comprehensive system of medicine, including acupuncture and herbs.

OTHER

Aura field: the energy cocoon which projects out from and surrounds the physical body.
Ayur-Vedic: East-Indian system of medicine.
Bioenergetics: a recently developed Western method of working with energy in the body and its relationship to psychotherapy – derived from the work of Wilhelm Reich.

Body-Energy systems: the various systems of energy in the body.
Body-energy: all forms and aspects of energy in the body.
Chakras: energy centres within the body.
Cultural Body-Energy Models: body-energy systems which have developed in a total cultural context.
Dynamic Meditation: a style of meditation which encourages the body to make spontaneous movement.
Energy-Body: the total of all of the body-energy systems – the Meridian System, the Chakra System and the Aura Field.
Gross anatomy: the material substance of the physical body.
Impersonal, Transpersonal: beyond the individual ego identity, and relating to the higher self.
Kundalini: a refined energy which ascends the spine in Yoga.
Metaphorical and Symbolic language: non-descriptive language understandable only to the initiated, and usually intended to protect the meaning of a statement.
Nadis: a network of energy lines in the Yoga system.
Nurse Healer: a nurse who practises Therapeutic Touch and hands-on healing.
Paranormal: beyond what is normal or usual.
Subtle anatomy / Energy anatomy: the structure of the energy system.
Therapeutic Touch: a contemporary Western title for a process which uses the hands as a focus to facilitate healing. The Western equivalent of Medical Chi Kung and Chi Kung Healing.

Further Information

THE INTERNATIONAL CHI KUNG/QI GONG DIRECTORY

The situation in the field of Chi Kung is growing and changing rapidly. To facilitate availability of information, and the healthy growth, spread and development of Chi Kung, we have established a continually updated database, network facility and mailing list. If you would like to receive a free Directory, get current updates, contribute information or be added to the Mailing List, please write, phone or Fax to:

The International Chi Kung/Qi Gong Directory
2730 29th St., Boulder, CO 80301, USA.
(303) 442–3131.

CLASSES AND TRAINING PROGRAMS

Apart from teaching a series of classes and training programmes at The Chi Kung School in Boulder, we offer workshops, training, seminars and talks elsewhere. This information and training is presented in a simple, straightforward language which makes it understandable, accessible and enjoyable for a wide range of people – oriental arts students, athletes, medical practitioners, dancers, health care providers, professional associations, community groups, business executives, senior citizens. These presentations are designed to be inspiring, instructive and fun, and can range from a one hour talk or presentation at a meeting or Conference, to a weekend (or longer) workshop.

For further information, write, phone or Fax to:

James MacRitchie
The Chi Kung School,
The Body-Energy Center,
2730 29th St., Boulder, CO 80301, USA.
(303) 442–3131.

TAPE CASSETTE OF THE EXERCISES IN THIS BOOK

In order to assist in the practice of the exercises in this book a special cassette tape has been produced which guides you through each exercise step-by-step, in order to get you to the point where you can then continue on your own. To obtain a copy of this tape send a cheque/money order for $13.00 U.S. (which includes postage) to the above address.

Useful Addresses

The following is a list of Resources for Chi Kung. It includes major organizations, teachers, contacts, networks, magazines and catalogues, for you to find out more. Each of the people or organizations listed here is known by the author, and comes highly recommended. This is not a comprehensive list – there are obviously many other teachers of high calibre not included here. Some people I contacted declined to be included. I hope that this helps get you connected and started, and then it is up to you to take it from there.

ORGANIZATIONS AND TEACHERS

USA

Organizations

China Advocates, 1635 Irving Street, San Francisco, CA 94122. 415–665–4505. Contact: Howard Dewar.

Chinese National Chi Kung Institute, P.O. Box 31578, San Francisco, CA 94131. 1–800–824–2433. Contact: Roger D. Hagood.

Qigong Academy, 8103 Marlborough Ave., Cleveland, OH 44129. 216–842–9628. Contact: Richard Leirer.

Qigong Human Life Research Foundation, P.O. Box 5327, Cleveland, OH 44101. 216–475–4712. Contact: Master Tian You Hao.

The Qigong Institute, East West Academy of Healing Arts, 450 Sutter St., Suite 916, San Francisco, CA 94108. 415–788–2227/323–1221. Contact: Master Effie Po Yew Chow or Dr. Kenneth Sancier.

Qi Gong Resource Associates, 1755 Homet Road, Pasadena, CA 91106. 818–564–9751. Contact: Shantika Lamanno.

Teachers

Master Mantak Chia, The Healing Tao, The Immortal Tao Foundation, P.O. Box 1194, Huntington, NY 11743. 516–367–2701. Fax 516–367–2754. Workshops and trainings are held internationally.

Master Bruce Kumar Frantzis, One Cascade Drive, Fairfax, CA 94930, 415–454–5243. Trainings also held in Boston, New York and England (see Brian Cooper).

Lawrence Galante, 209 1st Ave., New York, NY 10003. (212) 982 1484.

Dr. Roger Jahnke, Health Action, 19 East Mission #102, Santa Barbara, CA 93101, 805–682–3230. Fax 805–569–5832.

Mark Johnson, 3461 63rd St., Sacramento, California 95820. 1–800–497 4244.

Dr. Hong Xun Shen, in New York City – see Belgium

Charlotte Sun and Da-Jin Sun, Genesee Valley Daoist Hermitage, Box 9224, Moscow, Idaho 83843.

Gunther and Rylin Weil, Chi Kung and Corporate Training Associates, P.O. Box 2677, Aspen, Co 81612. 303–945–4050. Trainings also conducted in Europe for Corporate Executives.

Master Yan Xin, The International Yan Xin Qigong Association, c/o Tong-Yi Li, 218 Mansfield St., New Haven, CT 06511. Tel/Fax 203–498–9587.

Dr. Jwing-Ming Yang, Yang's Martial Arts Association, 38 Hyde Park Ave., Jamaica Plains, MA 02130–4132. 617–524–8892. Fax 617–524–4184.

Britain

London

Mark Caldwell – see Bristol.

Master Bruce Kumar Frantzis, c/o Brian Cooper, 85 Davey Drive, Brighton BN1 7BJ, East Sussex. 0273–506833.

Master Simon Lau, Eastern Horizon Studio, 28 Old Brompton Rd., South Kensington, London SW7 3DL. 071–581–1118.

Masters Zhi Xing and Zhen-Di Wang, The British Qigong College, 2 St. Albans Road, London NW5 1RD. 071–284–3673.

Master Lin Jun Wen, San Ling Clinic, 211 Archway Rd., Highgate, London N6 5BN. 081–347–8076.

Bristol

Mark Caldwell, The Healing Tao Foundation – England, 3 Redcliffe Parade East, Bristol BS1 6SW. 0272–268073. Fax 0272–225086. (Also sponsors Master Mantak Chia in England.)

Jeremy Ross, Greenfields Qigong Centre, 2 Rockleaze Ave., Sneyd Park, Bristol BS9 1NG. 0272–687777. Programmes also taught in Holland and Sweden.

Liverpool

Bill Harpe, The Blackie, Great Georges Community Cultural Project, Great George Street, Liverpool L1 5EW. 051–709–5109. (Classes and training for the general public.)

Manchester

Linda Chase Broda, The Village Hall, 163 Palatine Road, Manchester M20 8GH. 061–445–1568.

Danny Connor, The Qigong Institute, 18 Swan Street, Manchester M4 5JN. 061–832–8204.

Michael Tse, Tse Qigong Centre, P.O. Box 116, South D.O., Manchester M20 9YN. 061–434–5289.

Newcastle-on-Tyne
Bi Song Guo, 12 Church Lane, Gosforth, Newcastle-on-Tyne. 091–213–2464.

Sifu Peter Young, PE International, 176 Helmsley Road, Newcastle-on-Tyne NE2 1RD. 091–261–9777.

Reading
John and Angela Hicks, The College of Integrated Chinese Medicine, 40 College Road, Reading, Berkshire RG6 1QB. 0734–263366.

Scotland
Larry Butler, 5 West Bank Quadrant, Glasgow G12 8AF, Scotland. 041–334–5838.

Wales
Richard Farmer, Rising Dragon School, The White House, Maryland, Nr. Trellech, Monmouth, Gwent NP5 4QJ, Wales. 0600–860–305.

Europe

A number of the above teachers, in both Britain and USA, teach in Europe. Contact them as listed above for further information.

Belgium
Master Hong Xun Shen, Qigong Institute, Smidsestraat 172, 9000 Ghent, Belgium. 091–22–10–04 / Fax 091–21–74–55. Trainings also presented throughout Europe, and in New York City.

France
Dr. Vyes Requena, Institut European De Qigong, 13 Av. Victor Hugo, 13100 Aix En Provence, France. Tel: 33–42–26–98–82. Fax: 42–26–50–04.

International

Australia
Master Jack Lim, Qigong Association of Australia, 458 White Horse Road, Surrey Hills, Victoria 3127. 03–836–6961.

Canada

Master Shou-Yu Liang, Shou-Yu Liang Wushu Institute, 7951 No. 4 Road, Richmond, B.C., Canada V6Y 2T4. 604–228–3604. 604–273–9648.

China

The International Qigong Science Association, c/o Prof. Wang, Qi-Ping, Somatic Science Research Center, Dept. of Electrical Engineering, Xian Jiao Tong University, Xian, Shaanxi Provence, China 710049.

The World Academic Society of Medical Qigong, c/o Mr. Hua Yuan, He Ping Jie Beikou, Bei San Huan Lu 29, Beijing 100013, China.

China Wushu Association, #3 An-Din Road, Chao-Yang District, Beijing, China 100101. 491–2150.

New Zealand

David Hood, 341 Centaurus Rd., St. Martins, Christchurch 2, New Zealand. Tel/Fax 03–337–2838.

MAGAZINES AND CATALOGUES

INTERNAL ARTS CATALOG, P.O. Box 1777, Arlington, Texas 76004. Publisher: Dr. John P. Painter. 1–800–223–6984. Fax 817–460–5125.

QIGONG MAGAZINE, P.O. Box 31578, San Francisco, CA 94131. Publisher: Roger D. Hagood. 1–800–824–2433. FAX 415–992–4445.

QI – THE JOURNAL OF TRADITIONAL EASTERN HEALTH AND FITNESS, Insight Graphics Inc., Box 221343, Chantilly, VA 22022. Publisher: Steve Rhodes. 703–378–3859. Fax 703–378–0663.

REDWING REVIEWS, Redwing Book Company, 44 Linden St., Brookline, Massachusetts 02146. Publisher: Bob Felt. 1–800–873–3946. Fax 617–738–4620.

T'AI CHI, Wayfarer Publications, Box 26156, Los Angeles, CA 90026. Publisher: Marvin Smalheiser. 213–665–7773. Fax 213–665–1627.

Index

acupuncture 2, 16, 37, 38–9, 40, 45, 50, 75–6, 78, 100
aura field 95–6

basic substances 52–3

chakras 94–5
Chi Kung 3–6, 17, 25, 27, 45, 89, 104, 105
  and everyday life 14–15
  and other energy systems 91–2, 99–100
  applications of: for extraordinary abilities 79–80; for fitness 72–3; for immortality 82–4; for longevity 78–9; for sex 76–8; for spiritual development 80–2
  benefits 10–11
  different spellings 4
  distinguished from other exercises .21
  history of 32–4
  in modern times 37–40
  see also Nei Dan, Wei Dan
China, history of 25–8
choosing a teacher 106–9
conception meridian 42, 48, 64, 85, 88

Energy/Chi 1–2, 3, 9–10, 23–4, 27, 32, 34, 45, 46, 48, 49, 50, 51, 52, 55, 75, 76, 78–9, 109–13
  anatomy 46–57
  ancestral (yuan chi) 86
  body energy models 92–100
  cultivating 10, 33, 41–4, 68–9, 80, 81–2, 84–8, 101–3, 113–15
  negative 37, 41, 44, 65, 109
  physiology 57–69
  sensation 104
  system 15, 16, 46, 89–93
  time sequence 63–4
exercises
  1. the healing smile 22–4
  2. the energy shower 41–4
  3. focusing at your body centre 66–9
  4. knocking at the door of life 84–8
  5. energy recharge 101–3
  6. healing energy in your own hands 115–18

family relationships 62–3
five elements 58–60, 110

girdle meridian 48
governor meridian 44, 48, 64, 85–7, 88, 102
great envelope of the spleen 49

health 10, 14–15, 16, 75–6
factors of disease 64–5
'hierachy of control' 15, 46

internal ecology 60

Jing 55, 76, 77, 78, 79, 94

Lou channels 49

Mantak Chia 3, 12, 88
Martial arts 3, 9, 12, 20, 40, 73–5
meridians 40, 45, 46–9, 75, 89, 92, 93–4
see also under specific meridians
microcosmic orbit 48, 88, 113

natural cycles 65
Nei Dan 17–18, 22, 35, 66

organs or 'officials' 49–50, 51–2, 62–4

Pa Kua 66–9
paranormal abilities 79–8
points 50
Bai hai (meeting of the hundred) 42, 83, 102
Chi hai (the sea of Chi) 103
Da zhui (great hammer) 102, 115, 116
Luo gong (palace of weariness) 102
Ming men (door of life) 86–7
Shan zhong (within the breast) 102
Yin teng (original cavity of pure spirit) 103
Yong quan (bubbling spring) 102
practice 104–5, 109–13
precautions 105–6
pulses 51–2

Shen 55, 77–8, 79, 94
soul and spirit 55–6, 78
spiritual development 80–2
subtle anatomy 90

table of correspondences 60–1
Tai Chi Chuan 45, 74–5
Taoism 58, 62, 78, 81, 82
history of 28–32
therapeutic touch 3, 76, 98–100
three chou 50–1
three tan t'ien 54
three treasures 54–5
thrusting meridian 43, 48

Wei Chi 75, 94
Wei Dan 19–20, 35, 41, 75, 84, 101

Yang Qiao meridian 48
Yang Wei meridian 48, 49
Yin and Yang 57
the eight principles 58
Yin Qiao meridian 48, 49
Yin Wei meridian 48, 49
Yuan Chi 86–7